A TEXAS RANGER

by

N. A. JENNINGS

FOREWORD

by

J. FRANK DOBIE

INTRODUCTION

by

STEPHEN L. HARDIN

UNIVERSITY OF OKLAHOMA PRESS
NORMAN AND LONDON

Library of Congress Cataloging-in-Publication Data

Jennings, N. A. (Napoleon Augustus), 1856–1919.
    A Texas ranger / by N. A. Jennings ; foreword by J. Frank Dobie ;
introduction by Stephen L. Hardin.
        p.   cm.
    ISBN 0–8061–2903–4 (pbk. : alk. paper)
        1. Jennings, N. A. (Napoleon Augustus), 1856–1919.   2. Texas
Rangers—Biography.   I. Title.
    F391.J543 1997
    363.2'092—dc21   96-44442
    [B]   CIP

Permission by the J. Frank Dobie Estate to reprint the foreword in this edition
is gratefully acknowledged.

1   2   3   4   5   6   7   8   9   10

CONTENTS

CONTENTS

FOREWORD

". . . brought in the body of Pedro Paralis, a noted cow thief. He resisted arrest and died with a dozen bullet holes through him."

Thus reads the postscript to a letter signed "very respectfully" by L. H. McNelly, Captain of an independent company of Texas rangers, dated at Brownsville, December 5, 1875, addressed to his adjutant general, and now with other reports similarly laconic preserved in the State archives at Austin.

Although that postscript, representative in its nakedness, may be regarded as an item of history, from such materials alone a history that makes the past live could never be written. And if any time of the past was ever vivid and vital enough to live on through mere reporting—reporting without adornment or other adventitious trappings—it was the time when McNelly's rangers rode the bloody border of Texas. Hence it is exceedingly fortunate that a man who was to become a skilled reporter rode with them and later saw reason for putting down some of the things he had been a part of.[1]

Napoleon Augustus Jennings was born in Philadelphia, January 11, 1856. Most of his boyhood was spent at St. Paul's School in Concord, New Hampshire. Of the literature that he read and the motives that brought him to Texas at the age of eighteen, he has himself told. What happened to him during the next four years is a part of A TEXAS RANGER.

The death of his father in 1878 took him back to Philadelphia, where his family hoped that he would settle down to business. But the city seemed literally to smother him. Again he turned to the open ranges, this time in the far West. He rode as a cowboy; he drove a mountain stage; he prospected and mined; he painted signs and did other things. Again he returned to Philadelphia, to enter now on the profession that he was to die in, that of a newspaper man.

---

[1]For biographical material in the sketch that follows I am indebted to the widow of N. A. Jennings, Madam Edith Helena, Purdy Station, New York.

In 1884, at the age of twenty-eight, having already lived more positive days than most men live during a lifetime, he began work on the Philadelphia *News,* switched successively to the *Times* and *Tribune* of that city, next to the New York *Star,* and then, in 1887, to the *Sun,* which the genius of Charles A. Dana had made the lodestar of every ambitious reporter in America. Five years later he found himself on the staff of the San Antonio *Express*—a position that brought him again in contact with Texas rangers. Two years later he settled down for a long term with the New York *Evening World.* His fiery verses printed in newspapers during the Spanish American War won him the title of "the *automatic* poet." Meantime he had begun writing for the *Youth's Companion,* the *Saturday Evening Post,* and other magazines. He wrote anecdotes, for he was a fecund raconteur. He wrote stories of adventure, some of them designed especially for boys (like one printed in *St. Nicholas*) and all of them suitable for boys; the titles of two that appeared in the *Saturday Evening Post,* "A Dash for the Border" and "La Ley de Fuga," almost tell the story. He wrote biographical sketches; and one of them, "Lee Hall," about the famous Texas ranger who so influenced O. Henry, should be preserved. It appeared in the *Saturday Evening Post,* January 6, 1900.

Anecdotes of his facility as a reporter—and this is a striking quality in A TEXAS RANGER—yet linger. One night he was sent to interview Mark Twain. Other reporters presented themselves for the same purpose. But the great humorist was ill—very, very ill. He couldn't think of anything to say even if he felt like talking. Then Jennings asked if he might write an interview anyhow. "Go ahead, Jennings," Mark Twain replied, "for I am positive you wouldn't write anything I wouldn't say." The interview, which appeared in the New York *Evening World* next day, told how Mark Twain told about the cat that sat on the red hot stove lid—and the yarn is still repeated as one of Mark Twain's "characteristic" clinchings of a bit of philosophy.

While Roosevelt was police commissioner of the city of New York, Jennings had satirized him, but the career of the rough rider changed the journalist into an admirer and the two men became good friends. Indeed, during Roosevelt's race for governorship Jennings acted as his publicity agent.

During the first decade of the century Jennings toured Europe and the United States as press agent and manager for his wife,

Madam Edith Helena, operatic and vaudeville singer. The Madero Revolution, however, was too good for him to miss, and in 1910 he went to Mexico City on the *Herald* staff. During the World War his energies, like Roosevelt's, flared up once more— into words. He died December 15, 1919, in New York City.

Jennings belonged to the age of Roosevelt and Richard Harding Davis, and although he did not attain anything like an eminence comparable to that attained by either of those life-loving celebrities, it is hardly too much to say that the Strenuous One never wrote a history nor the great war correspondent a romance surpassing in sheer readableness A TEXAS RANGER. It appeared in 1899 with the imprint of Charles Scribner's Sons. Once, upon being asked why he had written it, Jennings replied: "I am a writing man; I needed money; I had a story to tell; I told it." Why the book has been allowed to run out of print is a puzzle; but why during recent years copies when available should have brought twenty-five or thirty dollars is not hard to explain. I defy anyone to read it without being engaged by its brightness and ranger-swift directness. The swing of young men in the saddle runs through the pages.

> "Then mount and away! give the fleet steed the rein;
> The ranger's at home on the prairies again."

Is the book true? The question is bound to be asked. The available muster rolls of McNelly's ranger company, which are by no means complete, show that N. A. Jennings certainly served from May 26, 1876, to February 1, 1877. In a letter written from New York City, dated July 7, 1899, to the widow of Captain McNelly (who married W. T. Wroe and now lives in Austin), Jennings comments on his newly published work thus: "In the book I made myself a member of the company a year before I actually joined. I did this to add interest to the recital and to avoid too much of a hear-say character. Told in the first person adventures hold the attention of the reader much more closely that at second hand."

Jennings himself, then, was not along when in June, 1875, "the McNelly men" laid out on the plaza in Brownsville—for whoever wanted to claim them—the bodies of thirteen Mexican bandits they had "naturalized"; nor was he, later on in the same year, with McNelly when that daring leader defied the United States government, crossed the Rio Grande, and fought the

Cortina raiders at Las Cuevas. Nevertheless, joining this extraordinary body of men some months later, Jennings scouted with them long enough to absorb their technique, their traditions, their spirit. If his own eyes did not see every act he has described, we may yet be sure that the stuff of his book, which is only incidentally autobiography, came to him from eye witnesses. He probably telescoped some events; space and the exigencies of narrative necessarily prevented his giving credit to every individual ranger who took part in the exploits recorded. Every writer who expects to be read must be selective, and many a historian who wanted to make the truth live has buried it in a dismal swamp of unselected facts.

Once I asked S. N. Hardy, a former McNelly ranger who served along with Jennings, this question:

"Did Jennings exaggerate the lawless conditions on the border in the seventies?"

"No," he replied, "it would be impossible to exaggerate the conditions. Why, when Dimmitt County—a part of the region where King Fisher's outlaws operated—was organized in 1880, only one man among the first set of county officials had not killed a man. That, though, does not mean they were bad men."

Then the veteran went on to relate an incident connected with Jesus Sandoval, the singular Mexican ranger whom Jennings describes so graphically in Chapter Ten. "One night while we were camped on the Rio Grande," Ranger Hardy relates, "I was in charge of the guard. Sandoval was keeping watch, and along about midnight I heard him cursing a blue streak in both Mexican and English. I went down to see what the trouble was. When I got near the river I saw an empty skiff, which had come over from the Mexican side. Also I saw Sandoval on his horse riding against a taut rope that was hitched to his saddle horn. The other end of the rope was tied to the neck of a Mexican. The Mexican's feet were tied to a mesquite bush. After Sandoval got through pulling, he dismounted and showed me another Mexican whose throat had been cut to the neck bone. He then explained that these two victims were the last of the gang who had burned his home and ruined his wife and daughter. I did not say anything about the matter to Captain McNelly until months later. Lots of things happened on the Rio Grande that never got into the ranger reports."

Down in the brush country between the Nueces River and the

Rio Bravo the tradition of McNelly's rangers is a part of the inheritance of the soil. Some of the people think that McNelly won the battle of San Jacinto! From what men who knew him say, McNelly was "hard." He made many a meal off nothing but mesquite beans. He slept many a night with nothing but a saddle blanket to protect him against mud and cold rain. He seldom, if ever, praised a man under him. If a man could not stand the gaff, was unfit to keep the pace, did not live up to the code, then he was discharged, usually "dishonorably." McNelly had little patience with failure to get an outlaw because of caution. At the same time he saw little use of risking a good ranger's life to arrest a moronic bad man—and a majority of the bad men were mental as well as moral degenerates—only to see him later released by an intimidated jury. Yet it was his duty to rid the country of the cut-throat element. There was a way. "Take no chances," he once said to Sergeant Armstrong. "Chance" was sometimes a synonym for "prisoner." On this particular occasion Armstrong and his detail of rangers took no chances; as a result either five or eight—authorities vary as to the number—outlaws awoke in the dead of night in their camp beside the Espantosa Lake to bite the dust. Regardless of the number, the riddance was good and was necessary to be accomplished in the way it was accomplished.

Yes, McNelly was a hard man—with outlaws. He lived in hard times. He had also the blood of Virginia chivalry in his veins. It is strange that a ranger and a gentleman in combination should be considered contradictory while "a soldier and a gentleman" is a commonplace. Let people who cannot understand the combination in "a ranger and a gentleman" read a little pamphlet written by Mrs. D. W. Roberts, wife of a ranger captain, on her experiences in a ranger camp. Let people who flinch at the idea of goriness and courtesy combined in a ranger read the lives "gay with gore" of such gallants as Sir Francis Drake. The rangers of Jenning's time were as a rule anything but ruffians, even though many of them had had their training on the frontier. They were hand-picked men, and a well bred youngster like Jennings was at home among them. They loved living.

When at the age of thirty-one, on September 4, 1877, L. H. McNelly, the intrepid ranger, died, the disease which took him off having been brought on by exposure in line of duty, he was buried in the village of Burton in Washington County, Texas, and Captain Richard King, representing the ranchmen of the border ranges, erected there a granite monument to his memory. It was a decent memorial, but it was not needed to keep the McNelly name green.

Although, like "cowboy," the word "ranger" was old long before English-speaking colonists crossed the Mississippi River, it remained for Texas to give both words the connotations they now bear. The body of writings connected with cowboys has grown to be rather voluminous. Cowboys rode from the Sierra Madre to the prairies of Alberta, from the coast of Oregon to the Eastern sweep of the Gulf of Mexico; they numbered thousands upon thousands. The Texas rangers never numbered above a few hundred at one time, as a usual thing not above a few score. Their range, wide as it was, was yet confined to the territory of the state they served. Considering their proud and far-flung reputation, the literature about them is exceedingly limited; a thorough history of the corps is yet to be written. It is a matter for genuine gratulation that, along with James B. Gillett's excellent SIX YEARS WITH THE TEXAS RANGERS, Jennings' A TEXAS RANGER is now made available for boys and men and women who like a brave, clean-cut narrative, simply and honestly told, about those brave and clean-cut frontiersmen, the Texas rangers.

J. FRANK DOBIE.

Austin, Texas
San Jacinto Day, 1930
(Revised March 16, 1936).

INTRODUCTION

For nearly a century, readers and critics have not known quite what to make of *A Texas Ranger* or its author Napoleon Augustus Jennings. In roughly equal measure they have lavished praise and heaped scorn on both. Bibliophile Ramon F. Adams, for example, thought so highly of the volume that he listed it in *The Adams One-Fifty: A Checklist of the 150 Most Important Books on Western Outlaws and Lawmen.* By contrast, in his classic book, *The Texas Rangers: A Century of Frontier Defense,* historian Walter Prescott Webb relegated Jennings to a single footnote. Yet, what a footnote it is. In it he condemned the book as one that "abounds in errors and misrepresentations" and castigated Jennings as a charlatan who made false claims regarding his participation in several key operations. Notwithstanding the conflict surrounding this reminiscence—and the accuracy of that designation is far from certain—it has gone through several editions, and Old West aficionados remain eager to add it to their collections.[1]

Immediately following its publication in 1899, questions arose regarding the book's authenticity. As J. Frank Dobie relates in the foreword to this edition, Jennings came to Texas in 1874 as a lad of eighteen. He joined Captain Leander H. McNelly's Special Force on May 26, 1876, and mustered out on February 1, 1877. Thereafter, he traveled back east, where he labored as a journalist and press agent. Jennings waited twenty-two years to record and publish the account of his time in South Texas, a gap that weakened the authority of his account.

He appeared to have served with McNelly, but in what capacity? George Durham, who undoubtedly functioned as a member of the Special Force and dictated *Taming the Nueces Strip: The Story of McNelly's Rangers*, lambasted Jennings's credibility:

---

[1] Ramon F. Adams, *The Adams One-Fifty: A Check-list of the 150 Most Important Books On Western Outlaws and Gunmen* (Austin: Jenkins Publishing, 1976), 50; and Walter Prescott Webb, *The Texas Rangers: A Century of Frontier Defense* (Boston: Houghton Mifflin, 1935), 265n.

> This Jennings was taken on at Laredo as a field clerk to do the writing. Later on he sure wrote. He sold stories on McNelly to a big magazine, and he put it in a book. The boy took it mostly out of his head, and it is pretty awful. For instance, he has Las Cuevas a one-day skirmish, with himself as Captain's right-hand man.

Jennings himself admitted taking liberties. Writing Mrs. Carey Cheek McNelly, the Captain's widow, he explained: "In the book I made myself a member of the company a year before I actually joined. I did this to add interest to the recital and to avoid too much of a hear-say character."[2] This disclosure does little to bolster the confidence of historians who must consider what else Jennings might have concocted to "add interest."

A Texas Ranger had its season and lapsed into relative obscurity, known to only a few specialists. In 1928, Leonidas Warren Payne, Jr., a cofounder of the Texas Folklore Society and English professor at the University of Texas, cited Jennings in *A Survey of Texas Literature*, along with the work of a colleague: "Professor Walter P. Webb of the University of Texas has in preparation an exhaustive history of the Rangers." Dr. Payne extolled Webb's manuscript as one that would prove an "authoritative contribution."[3] By then, Jennings's book had been out of print for years and had become quite scarce. It would have remained so had not Southwest Press of Dallas reprinted it in 1930 with a new foreword by an up-and-coming folklorist named J. Frank Dobie. The addition of this foreword caused a rupture in the friendship between Dobie and Webb, one of the most regrettable fallouts in the province of Texas letters.

Dobie and Webb considered themselves mavericks in academe and shared much in common, being the same age and both junior faculty members at the University of Texas. Their correspondence reveals that they had been soul mates for several years. In 1923, however, when Dobie refused to pursue the Ph.D. degree, he left to chair the English Department at Oklahoma A & M, in Stillwater. Throughout Dobie's self-imposed two-year exile, Webb remained a staunch friend. Webb pledged to do whatever he could to help Dobie return to Austin, but his own status was far from secure. Webb had written a master's thesis at the University of Texas in 1920, entitled

---

[2] George Durham as told to Clyde Wantland, *Taming the Nueces Strip: The Story of McNelly's Rangers* (Austin: University of Texas Press, 1962), 136; and Jennings quoted in John H. Jenkins, *Basic Texas Books: An Annotated Bibliography of Selected Works for a Research Library* (Austin: Jenkins Publishing, 1983), 282.

[3] Leonidas Warren Payne, Jr., *A Survey of Texas Literature* (New York: Rand McNally, 1928), 10.

"The Texas Rangers in the Mexican War." When he failed his Ph.D. comprehensive orals at the University of Chicago, however, he returned to Texas humiliated. There his mentor, Eugene C. Barker, obtained for him a post as associate professor at the University of Texas.[4]

Webb and Dobie understood that, without the advanced degree, they must secure their jobs through the sheer bulk and brilliance of their writing. Meanwhile, Payne worked behind the scenes, and in 1925 Dobie received the call to return. He still refused to earn a Ph.D., however, and instead began to grind out articles on regional culture and folklore for popular magazines and collaborated on his first book. Published in 1929, Dobie based *A Vaquero of the Brush Country* on the autobiographical notes of South Texas cattleman John Young.[5]

Dobie, of course, knew that since 1918 Webb had been researching a comprehensive history of the Texas Rangers. He was equally aware that his associate had pinned many of his professional hopes on its success. On Christmas Day, 1929, Webb had the Dobies to dinner and the two discussed the project at length. Early in February 1930, Webb discussed his developing ranger book with Dobie again, but observed that his friend had become "secretive." He wondered why.[6]

On or about February 20, he learned the cause. He received the notice from Southwest Press announcing their forthcoming reprint of Jennings's *A Texas Ranger*—with a new foreword by J. Frank Dobie. This bombshell shattered Webb. He lamented, "Here was a reprint of a book with almost the same title as mine, coming out under the mast of one whom I had considered a friend."[7]

Bewildered and devastated by what he considered unscrupulous

[4] For a solid biography of Dobie, see Lon Tinkle, *An American Original: The Life of J. Frank Dobie* (Boston: Little, Brown, 1978); for Webb see Necah Stewart Furman, *Walter Prescott Webb: His Life and Impact* (Albuquerque: University of New Mexico Press, 1976) and Necah Stewart Furman, "Walter Prescott Webb" entry in *The New Handbook of Texas,* vol. 6 (Austin: Texas State Historical Association, 1996), 862–63.

[5] Francis E. Abernethy, "James Frank Dobie" entry in *The New Handbook of Texas,* vol 2, 662–63.

[6] E. C. B. [Eugene C. Barker] to Webb, February 2, 1930, with explanatory typed note on same letter by Webb, dated February 25, 1930, in Archives and Manuscripts, Walter Prescott Webb Papers, Box 2M 254, Dobie Correspondence File, Center for American History, University of Texas at Austin (hereinafter cited as Webb Papers). See also Llerena Friend, "W. P. Webb's Texas Rangers," *Southwestern Historical Quarterly* 74 (January 1971): 312–13.

[7] Ibid.

conduct, Webb sought the advice of Barker. His mentor counseled him to simply ignore the action unless Dobie brought it up, and if he did, to mention that he wished he had not done the foreword and leave it at that. Barker, however, did not intend to ignore the situation. He acquainted Payne with the circumstances of the breach. Recall that in *A Survey of Texas Literature* two years before Payne had acknowledged Webb's "authoritative contribution." Payne summoned his protégé and strongly suggested that he mend fences with Webb.

On the morning of February 25, Dobie met with his disgruntled colleague. Webb attempted to "make the best of it," but Dobie's indifference cut him even deeper. He noted that Dobie had played innocent, "treating the whole matter as incidental, one that he had given little thought to." He irritated Webb further by reminding him of something he had forgotten: "[Dobie] told me in conversation that I gave him the copy of the book to read, the first he had ever seen." Webb was far from mollified, but realized he could do little but grit his teeth. "I followed Dr. Barker's advice," he fumed, "and told [Dobie] to go ahead [with the project]." Even so, Webb concluded his notes of the meeting with a poignant reproach. "I have never had anything to give me quite the shock that this affair did, and I still fail, in view of all our past relationships, to understand how Dobie could have done it."[8]

Did Webb have a right to be so indignant? Llerena Friend, who knew both individuals well, maintained Webb believed that he "had so completely identified himself with the Rangers that they were HIS." Obviously, no scholar can file claim to a subject and deny others trespass. Yet, that was not the source of Webb's animosity— it was more a matter of Dobie's deceitfulness. During repeated meetings, how could Dobie have failed to mention that he was working on a ranger project of his own? Webb had taught Dobie most of what he knew about Texas Rangers. He probably recalled the 1924 letter in which Dobie confessed to knowing little of the state's real history: "[I]f merely writing these legends was all, I would have a picnic. But I am stalled constantly on history!" The fellow who "stalled constantly on history" now professed to be an authority on Texas Rangers. When he finally read Dobie's foreword, Webb was no doubt hurt even more by the lack of an acknowledgment. Why did Dobie behave in such a clandestine manner? He likely anticipated Webb's reaction and wished to achieve a fait accompli before spring-

---

[8] Ibid.

ing the news. Did Dobie feel so pressured to add another publication to his vita that he was willing to risk Webb's friendship? One cannot know with certainty, but apparently so.[9]

In December 1932 Webb published his review of *A Texas Ranger* and implicitly revealed his hostility for Dobie's endorsement of the book. In the pages of *The Mississippi Valley Historical Review,* Webb rebuked both Jennings and Dobie. Webb thought the author disingenuous and self-serving: "Though Jennings was only eighteen when he reached San Antonio in 1874, his adventures for the next six months as told by himself would make the exploits of Jack Hays and Ben McCulloch for the same length of time pale and insipid." Still smarting from Dobie's affront, Webb denounced the foreword in caustic tones:

> Mr. Dobie's foreword deserves some attention. He had no trouble in recognizing that Jennings had told a good story, Crusoean though it be. He recognized that the story was of doubtful authenticity. . . . Mr. Dobie took some liberty with the only official document quoted in his nine-page foreword. He strikes the heroic note of the book by quoting a fragment of a sentence from one of Captain McNelly's letters. The quotation, lifted from its context, together with Mr. Dobie's comment that follows, leaves the impression that Captain McNelly, or perhaps one of his rangers, brought in the bullet-riddled body of a cow thief who had resisted arrest. What Captain McNelly clearly reported was that a deputy sheriff had brought in the body. Surely the Texas rangers achieved enough "on their own hook" without taking credit, even by implication, for deeds performed by their fellow peace officers. Mr. Dobie suggests that from such items alone "a history that makes the past live" could not be written. This raises a question as to how much information one would have to gather on the doings of deputy sheriffs in order to write a history of the Texas Rangers.[10]

More than sixty-five years later, the dispute seems little more than a footnote in the publishing history of *A Texas Ranger.* Still, the discord surrounding Dobie's foreword suspended one of the storied friendships of Texas letters. In time the two were able to put aside their differences and resume cordial relations. Afterward Dobie attempted to appease Webb with lavish praise of his Texas Ranger book. In his *Guide to Life and Literature of the Southwest,* Dobie

[9] Friend, "W. P. Webb's Texas Rangers," 312–13; and Dobie to Webb, February 6, 1924, in Webb Papers, Box 2M 254.

[10] Walter Prescott Webb, review of N. A. Jennings, *A Texas Ranger,* in *The Mississippi Valley Historical Review* 19 (December 1932): 424–26.

lauded Webb's book as the "beginning, middle, and end of the subject." Dobie acknowledged that he had written the foreword to the 1930 Southwest Press edition of Jennings's book, but listed it without further annotation. Nevertheless, Webb was never able to fully restore his former warmth of feeling, despite their association with a mutual friend, Roy Bedichek, a naturalist who brought Dobie and Webb together to forge a triumvirate of Texas literature.[11]

The huge response to the 1930 edition, along with Dobie's endorsement, assured *A Texas Ranger*'s status as a Texas classic. By 1936 the Southwest Press impression was into its third printing, which included Dobie's revised foreword. By 1946 the first edition had become so scarce it made its way into *Fifty Texas Rarities*. The compiler's annotations observed: "Jennings' book is a readable account of his life as a ranger in the late 1870's. It is, perhaps, the most absorbing personal account by a Ranger." *A Texas Ranger* was reprinted five times within the next fifty years by various publishers, and Texas bibliophile and rare-book dealer John H. Jenkins further enhanced its standing when he included it his *Basic Texas Books*. Neatly sidestepping discussions concerning reliability, Jenkins allowed that "this is one of the *most interesting* accounts of the life of the Texas Rangers in the late 1870's" [emphasis added].[12]

Notwithstanding its emerging status as a classic, the book still was the subject of controversy. Although Webb was its most prominent critic, he was not alone in casting doubts on the Jennings narrative. Walter S. Campbell (Stanley Vestal) cataloged the Jennings account in *The Book Lover's Southwest: A Guide to Good Reading,* but he was rather parsimonious with his approval. He declared James B. Gillett's *Six Years with the Texas Rangers* the "best of ranger autobiographies" but dispatched Jennings with a single word: "Readable." Did he have reservations concerning its credibility? Was he attempting to damn the book with faint praise? One can not say with confidence, for this laconic annotation raises more questions than it answers.[13]

In *Burs under the Saddle: A Second Look at Books and Histories of the West,* Ramon F. Adams believed the Jennings book to be an

---

[11] J. Frank Dobie, *Guide to Life and Literature of the Southwest, With a Few Observations* (Dallas: Southern Methodist University, 1943), 40. For the relationship between Webb, Dobie, and Bedichek, see Ronnie Dugger, ed., *Three Men in Texas: Bedichek, Webb, and Dobie* (Austin: University of Texas Press, 1975).

[12] *Fifty Texas Rarities* (Ann Arbor: The William L. Clements Library, 1946), 40; and Jenkins, *Basic Texas Books,* 280–84.

[13] Walter S. Campbell (Stanley Vestal), *The Book Lover's Southwest: A Guide to Good Reading* (Norman: University of Oklahoma Press, 1955), 78.

"excellent reminiscence by one of the noted Texas Rangers" but identified several errors in the account. Ranger Captain Lee Hall did not, for example, kill outlaw Sam Bass. Rangers of the Frontier Battalion under John B. Jones shot Bass on July 19, 1878, and he died two days later. Jennings mistakenly has Bass meet his end in August. He completely misconstrued the events surrounding the deaths of Texas shootists Ben Thompson and King Fisher. No evidence exists to support Jennings's assertion that the Taylor-Sutton Feud began in Georgia. He also advanced the old canard that Texas outlaw John Wesley Hardin shot a man for snoring. Jennings errs when he reports a $12,000 reward for Hardin advertised by Louisiana authorities. In truth, Hardin killed no one in that state and its officials never offered a bounty on his head. Finally, Adams avowed that Jennings also embellished the peculiar circumstances of Hardin's death.[14]

What should modern readers think of all this? The factual errors ought not astonish new readers. Considering the time separating the events from publication, the wonder is that Jennings got anything right. Did Jennings seek to elaborate his role in the famed events of Texas Ranger history? Undoubtedly, but probably no more than many other older rangers. Seasoned students of western history understand that artistic aggrandizement is just part of the terrain. As for the book's veracity: both admirers and detractors were correct. The virtues that attracted Dobie the folklorist—the "Crusoean" tale, colorful characters, and a sense of time and place—remain intact. The vices that repelled Webb the historian—the errors, the ego, and exaggeration—endure as well. Historians must exercise caution if they seek to employ Jennings as a source, but then their training teaches them to employ skepticism toward any participant reminiscence. Finally, there is a genuine need for the current edition. Nowadays even the numerous reprints demand a high price—when one can locate them.[15] Historians, bibliophiles, and all who stalk the scent of gun oil and saddle leather will thank the University of Oklahoma Press for making *A Texas Ranger* available to a new generation of readers. The debate continues.

STEPHEN L. HARDIN

The Victoria College
September 1996

---

[14] Ramon Adams, *Burs under the Saddle: A Second Look at Books and Histories of the West* (Norman: University of Oklahoma, 1964), vii, 296.

[15] Wright Howes, *Howes U.S.-iana Catalogue Prices* (Austin: Morrison Books, 1990), J100, listed copies for sale from $300 to $425.

A TEXAS RANGER

Chapter I

PUBLIC OPINION IN TEXAS

In the following story of those years of my life which were passed on the broad tablelands of Western Texas, I have endeavored to set down, plainly and truthfully, events as they actually occurred. I have always given the correct names of places, but in some instances have thought it proper to change the names of persons. During a recent visit to Texas, for the purpose of going over the scenes of the adventures of earlier days, I found a number of highly respected citizens, living exemplary lives, who had formerly been eagerly hunted by the officers of the law. It would be manifestly unfair to give their real names in this history, and so expose them to the criticism of their fellow-citizens at this late day. In other instances, however, where the male-factors are notorious, I have not hesitated to use real names.

In justice to the great State of Texas, I wish to say that the conditions which existed in the period embraced in this narrative have undergone a complete change, and that in no State in the Union is the law more respected than it is in Texas today.

It was in September, 1874, that I first visited Texas. I was eighteen years old, and had only a short time before left the famous New Hampshire school where I had been a pupil for a number of years. My father, a Philadelphia merchant, was very indulgent to me, and I had never been obliged to contribute a penny toward my own support. The reading of books of travel and adventure had roused in me a spirit of unrest, and I wanted to see the world.

Some copies of *The Texas New Yorker,* a paper published in the interests of some of the Southwestern railroads, came into my hands, and my mind was inflamed by the highly colored accounts of life in the Lone Star State. I read every word in the papers, and believed all I read. Since then I have learned that Colonel J. Armoy Knox, later of *Texas Siftings,* was one of the men who wrote the most lurid articles for *The Texas New Yorker.* I was a callow youth at the time, however, and had never met the genial Colonel. I should know better now than to take him so seriously, but his humor was all sober fact to me then.

After reading of the wild, free life of the Texas cowboy, I made up my mind that life would not be worth living outside of Texas. In a few years—or was it months?—I had the assurance of Colonel Knox's paper that, so surely as I went to Texas, I should be a cattle-king, the owner of countless herds of beeves and unlimited acres of land. I forget now just how I was going to acquire these without money or experience, but I know the Colonel made it all as plain as daylight to me then. As a "boomer" he was a glorious success.

About the first of September, then, I told my father that I had decided to try life in Texas, if he would give his permission. I said I knew that a fortune awaited me there, and I wanted to go and get it before someone else gobbled it up. To my vast astonishment, my father gave his consent, but said that if I went I must depend on my own exertions for a living. He suggested that my enthusiasm had obtained the upper hand of my judgment, but said that he would not stand in the way of my following my inclination to try a little out-door life and shifting for myself. He gave me his blessing and $100.

I started for Texas at once, my objective point being San Antonio. From there I intended to go farther West and find the site for my cattle-ranch. Of course, this sounds ridiculous, but it seemed quite feasible to me at that time. Many and many a young man has gone out into the West with such ideas in his head; just as many and many an immigrant has come to America with the expectation of finding money lying loose in the streets for him to pick up as he pleased.

At that time the railroad ran only to Austin, the capital of Texas, and about eighty miles from San Antonio. I went from Austin to San Antonio on top of a stage-coach. I had lived well on my journey, and when I came to pay my stage-fare I found that my supply of ready money was getting dangerously low. But I had bought a six-shooter and felt that I was a real Texan, which made me happy. When I arrived in San Antonio I had $3.25. I went to the Baker House, a second-class hotel on the

Main Plaza of the quaint old town. I was well dressed, and I had a sole-leather trunk filled with clothing, so, fortunately for me, I was not asked to pay for my board in advance.

My first week in San Antonio was one of real misery. I knew that I could not pay my hotel bill when it should fall due, but farther than that I did not know. For the first time I wondered how I was going to get out on the plains to start my cattle-ranch. How was I to get away? How could I pay my bill without money? What was I to do? What would become of me?

I was in my first serious predicament, and as unhappy a youth as could well be imagined. I thought with longing of the safety of my father's house, in Philadelphia, and heartily wished myself back there again.

My mind was not a bit relieved by an incident which occurred at the hotel, three or four days after my arrival.

I was sitting in the hotel office, wondering what I should do to get out of my trouble, when the proprietor, Baker—a big, heavy, broad-shouldered man, with a long, gray beard, which gave him a patriarchal appearance—walked in. He was greatly excited. He walked straight up to a young man who was sitting near me and caught him roughly by the collar.

"Here, you rascal!" he exclaimed, "I've found you out. You thought you could beat me, did you? Take that!"

Old Baker emphasized his words by hitting the young man over the head with a heavy cane. The blood ran down the man's face, and he struggled to get away. He finally succeeded in escaping from Baker and ran out of the hotel.

"I guess he won't try to beat a hotel out o' board and lodging in a hurry again," said old Baker, looking after him, with a grin.

Naturally, this assault made a deep impression upon me. I looked upon Baker with distrust every time he came near me, and felt like throwing up my arm to ward off a blow whenever he greeted me.

The end of my first week came all too soon, and the clerk handed me my bill; it amounted to $10.25. The extra quarter was for bringing my trunk from the stage office to the hotel. I had seventy-five cents in my pocket when I received the bill. I thought it well over, and then made up my mind to go to Baker and make a clean breast of the whole matter to him. It was not without many misgivings that I decided to take this course, but it turned out to be the best thing I could have done. Mr. Baker listened with patience to my rather lame explanation of why I could not pay the bill. I was so nervous that I was almost crying with mortification.

"Well, my boy," said the old man, kindly, when I had finished, "we must find something for you to do. How would you like to work on a ranch?"

I told him that I had come to Texas to work on a ranch. I was willing to do so for a short time, I said, until I learned something about the business, then I proposed to start a ranch of my own. He asked me if I had any capital in prospect, and I told him I had not. I was very young indeed in those days.

The upshot of our conversation was that he introduced me to one of his guests, a cattle-man named Reynolds, who owned a ranch in Atascosa County, south of San Antonio. Reynolds asked me if I had ever worked in Texas before, and when I told him I had not, he hesitated about employing me. I assured him that, although I had not worked in Texas, I was not a bit afraid of any kind of work, and only longed for the chance to show what I could do. This did not seem to impress him greatly, but he finally said he would give me a trial.

Mr. Baker said I could leave my trunk at his hotel until I was able to pay him what I owed. I thought this was very kind in him. My trunk, by the way with its contents, was worth about ten times the amount of his bill.

I was so elated over my good fortune that I started out that evening to "see the town," a thing I had not attempted before. The first place I went to was a Mexican gambling-room. There were several games of *monte* in progress. I had never seen *monte* played, nor any gambling for that matter, and I became greatly interested. At last I grew so fascinated that I ventured to bet seventy-five cents—my fortune—on the turn of a card. I regret to say, I won. I bet again and again, until I had won over twenty dollars. I kept on playing, with the inevitable result that I left the place penniless. For the first time in my life I was "flat broke."

Early the next morning I started with Reynolds for his ranch. He brought two little Texas ponies around to the front of the hotel, about sunrise, and told me I was to ride one of them. I was delighted. I had ridden a horse perhaps a dozen times in my life, and I thought I was an expert rider. But I had never ridden very far at a time, and when Reynolds said we should have to go thirty-five miles that day I had some misgivings as to how I was going to stand it. But I kept them to myself, and we started. Reynolds set the pace at that easy "lope" which the tough, wiry little Texas ponies can keep up hour after hour without showing fatigue. The motion was as easy as that of a rocking-chair, and I thought I should never tire of it. I did, though.

Long before we had covered the thirty-five miles I began to suffer. I had often heard the common expression about every bone in one's body aching; I had probably used it, carelessly, myself; but before I finished that ride I knew of a verity what it meant. Not only did every bone ache, but every muscle, and joint, and nerve in my body, from the crown of my head to the ends of my toes, was giving me excruciating pain. Every mile we covered added to my sufferings.

We stopped at noon to rest and eat and let the horses graze. When, after about two hours, Reynolds said it was time for us to be going on, it took real courage for me to get on that little mustang again. It was after dark when we at last reached Reynold's ranch. I tumbled from the pony's back more dead than alive, and I then and there resolved never again to ride a horse. I was far too tired and in too much pain to sleep, and all night I suffered intensely.

Before I left Texas, I practically lived on a horse for three years. I have ridden for three weeks at a time in pouring rain, and have slept every night during that period on wet ground, covered with a wet blanket. I have ridden "bucking broncos," and horses that trotted with the gait of an animated pile-driver. I have raced for my life in front of a herd of stampeded cattle. I have been chased forty miles at night by desperadoes, anxious to make a sieve of my body with bullets. But never have I experienced anything like that first Texas ride.

Long before daylight the next morning I was called by Reynolds, who said that he wanted me to go to Pleasanton with him to a "stock meeting." I didn't know what a "stock meeting" was, but I was quite sure I didn't want to go to that one. I simply wanted to lie quiet and die, but pride came to my aid and, stiff and sore as I was, I struggled to my feet, ate a breakfast of black coffee and corn-bread, and again mounted my mustang. We started just as the first faint streak of dawn showed in the sky and reached Pleasanton about an hour after the sun had risen. Reynolds probably came to the conclusion that I was too much of a "tenderfoot" or "short-horn" for his use, for he deserted me in Pleasanton, and left me there to shift for myself. He calmly told me he had changed his mind about employing me, and went away and left me, taking with him the horse I had so painfully ridden.

Chapter II

CATTLEMEN AND THEIR CHEERY CUSTOMS

I had been in a sad predicament in San Antonio, but now my situation was indeed desperate. I was not only penniless, but hungry and friendless. The town was full of cattle-men and cowboys, who had come to it to attend the stock-meeting. They were a good-natured, jolly set of fellows, but through my inexperienced young Eastern eyes I saw in them only a lot of rough, loud-talking, swearing ruffians.

At that time Texas had but few fences in it, and cattle roamed at will all over the State. The only way a cattle-owner had of keeping his property was by branding the calves and cutting their ears in some fanciful way. These brands and ear-marks were duly registered in the county clerk's office and determined the ownership of the cattle. All unbranded cattle were known as "Mavericks." They belonged to nobody in particular, but if a cattle-man came across one, he would "rope" it, throw it down, and brand it.

The principal market for Texas cattle was in Kansas, and the cattle-men would gather great herds and drive them up through the Indian Territory to Kansas, where they would sell them. The cattle-men did not necessarily confine themselves to driving their own cattle, but would take those belonging to others as well. They were supposed to keep a careful record of all such cattle they had taken up and sold, and to make a settlement at a "stock meeting" every three months. As a rule, the cattle-men were not any too honest in keeping their records, and the stock meetings were in the nature of a farce. Very little money ever changed hands. The owner of a brand would meet the owner of another and say to him:

"Jim, I took up twenty-one o' your cows an' sold 'em. I'll give ye an order to take up twenty-five o' mine if ye ain't took up any lately."

"Well, I did round up sixteen o' your 'B T' brand," the other would reply, "so I reckon we can fix up the difference all right."

The chances were that both men were lying outrageously as to the number of cattle each had sold belonging to the other, but as all were doing the same thing, it was pretty thoroughly understood that the smartest man in gathering stock was the one to come out ahead.

Under no circumstances would a cattle-man ever kill any of his own stock for beef. He invariably hunted up for that purpose some brand which did not belong to him, and it was an unwritten law that cattle killed for beef should not be accounted for at the stock meetings. Some of the large cattle-owners actually advertised in the little county newspapers the brands which they wished other ranch-men to use for beef.

I am not exaggerating when I say that at that time in Texas ten times more cattle were stolen every year than were bought and sold. A man would acquire possession of a few cattle of a certain brand and would forthwith gather all cows and steers of all brands he could round up, drive them to Kansas, and sell them. Very often there were fights about the cattle and, as every man carried a six-shooter in that country, "killings" were of somewhat frequent occurrence. Still, there was a difference between a regular cattle-man and a common cattle-thief. The former always was the legal owner of at least one brand; the latter owned none at all.

My predicament at being thrown on my own resources among these rough-and-ready frontiersmen was, as may be imagined, a serious one. I was desperate. I hung around the stable where a good many of the stock-men put up their horses, and asked one after the other if he did not wish to employ me. I was not the sort they wanted, however, and I met with no success. I had about given up hope when the proprietor of the stable came to me and asked me if I didn't want to go out into the yard and draw water from the well for the horses. He said he would give me a dollar if I would draw water for two hours.

I had never done any hard work in my life, but I jumped at the opportunity that time. The yard was filled with horses, and close to the well was a trough for their use. They crowded around the trough and fought to get the water I drew from the well in buckets and poured into it. My position was dangerous and I fully realized it; in fact, I probably magnified it, for I was unused to being with horses.

I worked hard, however, and to such good purpose that in

half an hour I had exhausted the well. The stable-man acted handsomely. He paid me the dollar, although I had worked but half an hour. Later in the day I worked again for him, and that night he let me sleep in his hayloft.

For two weeks I worked around the stable and at other odd jobs in the little town, chopping wood and doing anything I could get to do, and I managed to make a bare living, but no more.

Then it was that I first met John Ross. He was a big-hearted, bluff Scotchman, with a bright red beard and the broadest of Scotch accents. He had come to Texas from Glasgow and had married a young San Antonio girl of good family, the granddaughter of José Antonio Navarro, one of the heroes of the Texas revolution. To this day, I look back with feelings of deepest affection and gratitude to these good people, for they were father and mother to me when, as a youth, I was alone in Texas and friendless.

Ross entered into conversation with me in Pleasanton and said he would take me to his ranch on the Atascosa Creek, about eighteen miles from Pleasanton, and give me work. He said he could not afford to pay much at first, but would give me board and lodging and enough to keep me in tobacco. He took me to the ranch in his wagon.

The first day he set me to work digging post-holes for a new fence he was building; but he was not a hard master, and when he saw I was getting tired he sent me to the creek to catch some catfish, a form of labor which was much more to my taste.

I helped Ross on his farm for three months, and gradually became used to harder work than I had ever supposed I could stand. It even became easy for me to get up before daylight and to go to bed with the chickens. My muscles hardened, and I learned how to use them to the best advantage, not easy knowledge to acquire when one is city bred and has lived an idle life.

At the end of three months Ross told me he had decided to go to Laredo, a town on the Rio Grande about one hundred and twenty miles south of his ranch. He said that he was going to cultivate a market-garden there, and that if I could raise about three hundred dollars he would take me in as a partner. I wrote to my father that I had a fine chance to go into business and he kindly sent me the three hundred dollars by return mail, together with a letter filled with loving advice. I fear I did not appreciate the advice nearly so much then as I do now, looking back from the standpoint of a man of experience. This is a veracious tale, however, and I am in duty bound to tell exactly what became of that money.

We started for Laredo early one morning in January, 1875. In the big covered farm-wagon were Mrs. Ross and "Tommy," the baby, the same who lately won distinction in a Texas Ranger company by hunting down desperate characters near Corpus Christi. Will Ross, John's brother, rode on horseback, as did I. I had about all the money in the outfit. We were fairly well armed, for the country was not free from Indians at that time and their raids from Mexico were quite frequent.

Never shall I forget that trip to Laredo, for I suffered much on it, physically and mentally. The weather was very trying for one so new to the country as I. The days were extremely warm and the nights uncomfortably cool. During the day the sun blazed in the heavens and his rays beat down on our heads with tropical force, but no sooner did the shades of night come on than the air grew icy cold, and before morning it was freezing. Two hours after the sun arose the next day, the terrible heat began again. To add to the discomfort of these extreme changes in temperature, water was very scarce and rattlesnakes extremely plentiful.

It was on this journey that I first experienced a Texas "norther." It came upon us early one afternoon. Will Ross and I were riding about a mile ahead of the wagon. We were coatless, and our shirts were open at the throats, for the heat was stifling. Suddenly, without the slightest warning, an icy wind swept across the prairie from the north. It chilled us, through and through, in a few seconds.

"Hello! a norther's coming," said Will Ross. "We'd better go back and get our coats."

We turned back to the wagon, but when we attempted to ride in the teeth of that terribly cold wind, we suffered so that we gave up the attempt. We dismounted and stood in the lee of our horses until the wagon came lumbering up. Then we bundled into our coats and overcoats and rode on to a creek, a mile or so ahead. There, under the shelter of one of the banks, we built a great fire and went into camp, to remain until the "norther" should blow itself out. This, Ross knew from experience would be in two days.

A "norther" invariably blows from the north for twenty-four

hours. Then it comes back, almost as cold, from the south for twenty-four hours more. The third day there is no wind, but the cold continues, gradually abating until, on the fourth day, the temperature is what it was before the "norther" came. I have been in New Hampshire when the thermometer marked forty degrees below zero; I have passed a night, lost in a snowstorm, in the Rocky Mountains in Colorado; but never have I suffered so from the cold as I have in a Texas "norther." One's blood gets thin in a warm climate, and it is not so easy to resist cold as in Northern latitudes. Not infrequently thousands of cattle will die, frozen to death, in a Texas "norther." During the winter months the "northers" sweep over Texas about once in every two or three weeks.

Lawrence Christopher Criss, on old Texas guide and buffalo-hunter, is responsible for the following tale of a "norther." Criss vouched for the absolute truth of it, and even offered to take me to the spot where it happened and show me the ashes of the camp-fire to prove it.

"It was along in the winter of '69 that I was out huntin' buffalo with a little hunch-back we called Twisted Charley," said Criss, telling me the yarn one night, sitting by a camp-fire near El Paso, Texas. "We were up in the Panhandle, and dead oodles of buffalo grazed around us. We had run across a herd in the afternoon, and killed nineteen between us. Twisted Charley and I were skinnin' them, and were takin' off the hides of four or five when the worst norther I ever remember struck us.

"We piled all the wood we could find on the fire, but we couldn't begin to keep warm, and when night come on it got colder, and colder, and colder, till the coffee, boilin' in the coffee-pot on the fire, had a skim of ice on it that we had to break before we could pour the coffee out.

"Well, a bright idea struck me, and I took one of the green buffalo-hides and wrapped myself up in it, and in a minute I was as warm and comfortable as a man could wish to be anywhere. You know there's nothin' warmer than a buffalo-hide, and this one was extra thick. Charley saw what I had done, and he went and got a hide, too, and wrapped himself up in it. We were not long in fallin' asleep after that, and I was peacefully dreamin' about skinnin' Jacarilla Apache buck Injuns to make moccasins out of, when, all of a sudden, I was woke up by the most awful howlin' I ever heard.

"I was sure the Injuns were down on us, and I jumped up and grabbed my rifle in a hurry. Then I saw that it was Twisted Charley who was doing the yellin'. I went over to where he lay, wrapped up in the green buffalo-hide, and I gave him a kick to wake him up, for I thought, of course, he had a nightmare.

" 'Help me out, help me out!' he yelled.

" 'What's the matter with you?' I asked.

" 'Don't you see I'm froze up in this hide and can't get out?' he howled.

"I took hold of the hide and tried to unroll it, but it was froze 'round him as hard as boiler-iron. He was warm enough, for he had wrapped himself in it with the hairy side next to him, but he wanted to get out bad.

" 'I can't unwrap that hide any way,' I said, after I'd made a trial at it.

" 'Cut it open,' said Twisted Charley.

"I took my skinning-knife and tried to cut it, but the hide was so hard it turned the knife-edge.

" 'I'll have to give it up,' I said, at last.

" 'What?' yelled Charley. 'Man, I can't stay in this hide forever.'

" 'You won't have to,' I says; 'this norther'll blow itself out in three days, and then you'll thaw out naturally.'

" 'Thaw me out at the fire,' said Charley.

"That seemed reasonable, and I rolled him over by the fire and began toastin' first one side and then the other. I thought I'd never get him out; but after awhile, when the hide was actually roasted, I managed to unroll it enough for him to get out. He sat up by the fire the rest of the night, swearin'. He was a beautiful swearer, and the air moderated a whole lot while he was sittin' there inventin' new oaths and lettin' 'em out."

There was one other thing which I did not particularly fancy on that trip to Laredo, and that was the howling of the coyote wolves around our camp at night. Any Texan will tell you that a coyote is the most cowardly and harmless of animals, but his howl is bloodthirsty and horrible at night. It is a shrill, wild, piercing yelp, tapering off to a long, dismal howl. There is something very human in it, and yet it is weird and uncanny and creepy, especially when the one listening to it is a young and inexperienced man, fresh from the quiet of Philadelphia streets.

Even when one becomes quite used to it, the howling is anything but soothing to the nerves.

Many a night on that trip I was kept awake for hours by the little wolves around the camp, for I could but believe they would attack us, there seemed such a menace in their howling. The others in the camp, including Mrs. Ross and her baby, paid no attention to the coyotes.

We arrived in Laredo, at night, about ten days after we had started, and found the little town in gala attire. The annual *fiesta,* or fair, was in progress in Nueva Laredo, just across the Rio Grande, in Mexico. The Mexicans of both towns had given themselves up to the enjoyment of the holiday season, and only *monte, mescal, fandangos,* bull-fights, and general hilarity were in order. *Mescal,* by the way, is a liquor made from the century-plant, and is about as strong as "moonshine" corn whiskey. It has a smoky taste which, to the American palate, is not very agreeable.

When we entered the town that night, the inhabitants were all out of doors and enjoying life to the utmost. At that time Laredo—now an important railroad terminus of twelve or fifteen thousand inhabitants—had about three thousand Mexicans and about forty Americans for its population. Of course, it was "run" by Mexicans. It was on American soil, but in its make-up and system of government there was little or no difference between it and the lesser town of Nueva Laredo, on the Mexican side of the river. We arrived in town about seven o'clock in the evening and, after a supper of *chili con carne* and *tamales,* we crossed the Rio Grande to see what we could of the *fiesta.*

The market plaza in the Mexican town was given up to the fair. It was filled with booths, and there were enough games of chance and wheels of fortune in operation to stock a dozen county-fair race-tracks in this country. In a big adobe building on one side of the plaza a great game of *monte* was in progress. On a long table extending down the middle of the main room in this building were many stacks of Mexican silver dollars. Smaller heaps of half-dollars and quarters were scattered here and there on the table. There were about five thousand silver dollars on the table, and I was told the bank was good for any amount up to fifty thousand dollars.

The dealers sat at intervals around the table, and between them were the players, who crowded around three or four deep.

The players wore gayly striped blankets thrown gracefully over their left shoulders. Nearly all wore enormous *sombreros,* wide of brim, and with high peaked crowns, and covered, in many instances, with a wealth of silver or gold lace and embroidery.

Every man in the room was smoking a cornhusk *cigarito.* I was impressed by the cold-blooded way in which they played the game. Win or lose, they displayed absolutely no emotion. They watched the dealer closely with their keen black eyes from under their wide hat-brims, as he turned up the cards upon which so much depended; but, no matter whether they became richer or poorer by the turn, they gave no sign of excitement.

One old fellow I watched losing steadily for fully half an hour. He calmly smoked his *cigaritos* as he continued to stack up his silver dollars, fifty at a time, and he seemed to regard the outcome with utter indifference. He had a well-filled wallet, and time after time he took bills from it, and had them changed by an attendant into silver to bet on the game. Only silver was allowed on the table. After a time, this old man began to win as rapidly as he had lost, but there was no change in his demeanor. He seemed devoid of nerves. He was an ideal gambler, but he was only a type of all the others.

From the fascination of watching others to the excitement of playing was a very little step and I took it. I came out of the room about fifty dollars poorer than I entered it. I had become separated from the Ross brothers, and I started around the plaza to hunt them up.

I had not gone far before I found myself surrounded by a crowd of half-drunken Mexicans. They were drinking *mescal* from a bottle. I attempt to pass on, but one of them caught me by the coatsleeve and detained me. I have no doubt whatever now that he merely wanted hospitably to invite me to take a drink from the bottle, but at that time I did not understand the language, and the low-browed, black-eyed, blanketed Mexicans looked so villainous that I feared I was about to be assaulted and robbed.

I still had over $200 of the $300 which I had intended to put into the vegetable gardening business with Ross, and when that Mexican caught hold of me and held me, I was frightened. I was so frightened, indeed, that I did a very foolish thing. I roughly broke away from him. He reached to catch me again, and I turned and hit him in the face. Then I ran.

How I escaped from that crowd and away from the plaza

has always been a puzzle to me, but I know that I found myself running as fast as I could go down the long street which led to the little ferryboat which was punted across the river between the two republics. Behind me, I knew there was a crowd of irate Mexicans, bent on capturing me, and wreaking vengeance for the insult I had put upon their companion and countryman. I flew on the wings of fear, for I doubted not that my fate would be sealed if they caught me. Suddenly, to my great horror, I felt myself caught around one arm by such a powerful hand that my progress was instantly arrested, and I was swung about as though I were on a pivot. Before I realized what had happened I heard a drawling voice say:

"You seem to be in a hurry, friend; where are you bound for?"

My captor was a superb-looking fellow. He was over six feet in height, and built like an athlete. His handsome, manly face was smiling good-naturedly. His mouth was hidden by an enormous drooping light moustache, but his blue eyes twinkled in evident enjoyment of my discomfiture.

He wore a big, wide-brimmed white felt hat and a richly embroidered buckskin Mexican jacket, and he was puffing a *cigarito*.

"Let me go! Let me go!" I cried. "A crowd of Mexicans are after me, and if they catch me, they'll kill me."

"What do they want you for?" he asked, in his drawling, amused tone.

"I hit one of them; and——"

"Oh, well, I reckon we can stand 'em off," he said. "Here, take this gun, an' use it."

As he spoke he handed me a six-shooter. By this time the advance runners of my pursuers had nearly reached the spot where we stood, under the flaring lamp in front of a saloon. My new friend whipped out the mate to the revolver he had given me, and fired straight at the rapidly approaching men. They turned, instantly, and ran the other way. I think they went a little faster than they had come. Then the big man, who had so strangely come to my rescue, smiled again, in his quiet way, and, putting up his six-shooters, said:

"Come in and have a drink; it'll do you good."

"Hadn't I better get over to Texas?" I inquired, anxiously; "those Mexicans may come back here at any moment."

"Oh, I guess they ain't in any hurry to come back, yet awhile," he answered. "If they do, we can have some more fun with 'em."

So I went into the saloon with him and took a drink of the vilest whiskey that ever passed my lips. I got away as soon as I could, and reached the ferry and the Texas side of the river without further adventure. Not, however, until I reached Ross's wagon, which he had put in a wagon-yard, did I feel quite safe.

The name of my friend in need was Thompson—Bill Thompson. He was a brother of the notorious Ben Thompson, the desperado marshal of Austin, Texas, who, with King Fisher, another desperado, was killed in San Antonio one night by William H. Simms, whom they attacked. But I shall tell their story further on. Bill Thompson, at the time he helped me, was a fugitive from justice, charged with killing a man in Kansas. There was a reward on his head of $500. In another place I shall also tell how, as a Texas Ranger, I was able to repay Bill Thompson for what he did for me that night.

CHAPTER III

I BECOME A QUARTERMASTER'S CLERK FOR A BRIEF SEASON

John Ross met with many disappointments in Laredo in his attempt to start a market-garden, and in the end gave it up. In the meantime my money was used up, and when at last we found the scheme was a failure I was down to my last ten dollars. I saw that I should have to look about for some way in which to make a living, and the outlook in that town of Mexicans was not bright.

I made the acquaintance of all the white men in the town, however, and among others I came to know a certain lieutenant of the Twenty-fourth Infantry, two companies of which regiment were stationed at Fort McIntosh, about a mile from Laredo and above it, on the Rio Grande. The lieutenant was the Quartermaster of the post and had an office in Laredo. He came to it from the post every morning. I heard he was in need of a clerk and I applied for the place. I was probably the only applicant he had, for he took me immediately.

I soon learned the routine of the office and found the work easy. But I did not keep the place long. The Quartermaster, like many other officers stationed at remote frontier posts, was not so abstemious as he might have been. In the mornings he was quite sober, but after he went to luncheon he wasn't. One afternoon he signed a number of reports which I had prepared, and told me to send them off. He did not so much as glance through the reports when he signed them, in an unsteady hand, and I was not certain they were correctly made out. I was new to the business and did not want to get into trouble, so I held the reports until the following morning, with the idea that he would look them over when he was fresh and clear-headed. That was where I made a mistake. He was furiously angry when I delicately hinted, the next morning, that he had been slightly under the influence of intoxicants the day before.

"Make out a voucher for your pay to date, instantly, sir," he said, gruffly. "You are grossly impertinent, sir."

I did not think I had been impertinent in trying to avoid

trouble for him, but he would listen to no explanation, and I had to go.

There was one curious thing which happened while I was a quartermaster's clerk and which may be worthy of brief mention. In the same building with the Quartermaster's office was the store-room of the commissary department. It was filled with all sorts of canned goods and glass jars containing preserves, jams, pickles, butter, and fancy groceries of many kinds. One day word came that the Inspector-General was about to pay the office a visit. The Quartermaster received the letter and gave it to me to file. He told the Commissary-Sergeant about it.

About an hour later there was a great crash in the store-room next to the Quartermaster's office. We ran in to see what was the matter, and found that all the shelves on one side of the room had broken down, carrying with them the glass jars. Butter, pickles, preserved fruits, jams, olives, and the like lay in a heap on the floor, mixed up with broken glass. When the Inspector-General arrived, the next day, he looked long and earnestly at the wreck and then condemned the whole lot to be thrown into the Rio Grande. The accident seemed a most timely one, for the Commissary-Sergeant had been doing a thriving little retail grocery business among his acquaintances, before the Inspector-General's visit.

After leaving the Quartermaster's service, I was again thrown on my own resources, and it was at this time that I first met Hamilton C. Peterson, United States Commissioner at Laredo. Peterson had formerly been a captain in the army. He was a good lawyer and an expert civil engineer. He was the best revolver-shot I ever saw before or since. He was always ready to bet anything, from a drink of whiskey to a basket of champagne, on his marksmanship. He could hit a half-dollar with a pistol-ball four times out of five at fifty paces.

Physically, Peterson was a fine-looking man. His face was handsome, and his big, fierce, black mustache gave the impression that he was a dare-devil of the most pronounced type, shading, as it did, a resolute, well-modelled chin. His appearance did not belie his character. His principal occupation, at the time I first made his acquaintance, was challenging men to fight duels. He was a hard drinker, and very quarrelsome when in liquor. Every time he had a dispute with a man, he would, as soon as possible thereafter, challenge him to fight a duel. Sometimes he would get me to write a challenge at his dictation. But as the fame of his marksmanship had spread all over the State, his challenges were never accepted.

When I left the Quartermaster I went to Peterson and asked him if he could get me something to do. He said he could and would. He was going on a surveying trip in a few days, and would take me with him to carry a surveyor's chain and to assist him in other ways. Having decided this important matter for me, he proposed that we go and play a game of billiards. We did so, and it was not until midnight that we started for Peterson's little adobe, one-roomed house, to which he had invited me as his guest until he should be ready for the surveying trip.

On the way to the room, a cat ran across the street in front of us. It was too good a chance for Peterson to miss trying his marksmanship, and he pulled his six-shooter and blazed away at the cat. The animal gave a yowl and disappeared in the darkness. We continued up the street, but had not proceeded far before we found ourselves surrounded by a number of Mexicans. With them was the city marshal, a stalwart young man named Gregorio Gonzales. His companions were Mexican policemen. They at once put us under arrest for shooting in the street, but Peterson managed to throw his pistol away in the dark before they could search him.

I had a sword-cane in my hand, but they did not know it was aught but a plain, ordinary walkingstick. Despite Peterson's protests, they took us to the house of a magistrate named Sixto Navarro, an uncle, by the way, of Mrs. John Ross. It was nearly one o'clock in the morning when we reached Senor Navorro's house. The magistrate said he was willing to let us go on our own recognizances until morning, but City Marshal Gonzales insisted that we be made to give bonds for our appearance, or else spend the rest of the night in the "calaboose."

"But I am the United States Commissioner, and you know I am not going to run away," said Peterson. "Let this young man and me go for the night and I give you my word of honor that we will be on hand whenever you say in the morning."

Senor Navarro was willing, but Gonzales was obdurate, and at last Peterson had to send for a friend and give the required bail. It was fixed at $300 each.

As soon as we were liberated, we went to Peterson's room. He was as mad as a hornet. He lighted a lamp and began to rummage over a lot of papers which he took from his desk. At last he selected one and, turning to me, he said:

"Here, my boy, I want to swear you in as a special Deputy United States Marshal. I have some work which must be done to-night, and you must do it."

"What kind of work?"

"Why, I want you to execute *capiases* on Gregorio Gonzales and Sixto Navarro. Navarro could easily have let us go if he had really wanted to do it. I have affidavits here that both of them have been smuggling goods across the Rio Grande from Mexico. I will make out the *capiases* for them, and I want you to arrest them. You have the right to summon as big a posse as you think you need in making the arrests, and the *capiases* call for their bodies, dead or alive. When you have arrested them, bring them here and I'll show you some fun."

It looked as though I was going to have some "fun" in the execution of those *capiases*. But I consented to be sworn in as a special Deputy Marshal.

"Now," said Peterson, when he had administered the oath, "you go across the street and wake up St. Clair and his partner and take them along with you to help make the arrests."

St. Clair and his partner were sign-painters, who had wandered into Laredo looking for work, and had been kept busy repainting the sacred figures in the church. The shop was usually half full of saints in all stages of dilapidation. St. Clair, whose bump of reverence was not very strongly developed, used one of the figures for a hat-rack, and the effect was startling.

I went across the street and aroused the painters, who at once entered into the spirit of the thing, and declared they were ready to kill Gonzales and the whole Mexican police force, if necessary. As soon as they were dressed, we started off to find the city marshal.

We didn't have far to go. We found him in a bar-room, in the middle of a graphic description to a number of Mexicans of the way he had arrested Peterson and me and taken us before Navarro. He seemed surprised to see me walk in with St. Clair and his partner, but he was still more astonished when I walked up to him and, touching him on the arm, said:

"I have a *capias* for your arrest. My orders from the United States Commissioner are to take you before him, dead or alive. You'd better come quietly and avoid trouble."

"Wha—what do you want me for?" he gasped while his companions looked on in wonder.

"You are wanted for violating the revenue laws of the United States," I answered in as harsh a voice as I could assume. "The *capias* will explain that, if you care to read it."

"But you are not an officer."

"I am a United States Deputy Marshal. Come, I haven't time to stand here talking to you. I arrest you, and if you don't come quietly, I will use force to make you."

He saw that I was in dead earnest, and he had too much respect for the law to think of disobeying the mandate of an officer armed with a *capias* and backed by a posse and six-shooters. He hesitated no longer, but came at once, followed by the men who had been listening only a few minutes before to the story of Peterson's arrest. Peterson's office was near by, and in a very few minutes we were there. The Commissioner was seated at his desk. He wore an exprssion of great solemnity. Entirely ignoring the presence of the city marshal, he turned to me and said:

"Mr. Marshal, you will please open my court."

I stepped to the door, and called out in a loud voice:

"Oyez, oyez, oyez. The Honorable United States Commissioner's Court for the Western District of Texas is now open. All persons having business with said court draw near and ye shall be heard."

I had never opened a court before, but I thought that was about the right thing to say. Having startled the night air of the sleeping town, I went back to Peterson's desk.

"Mr. Marshal," said he, "you have brought a prisoner into court."

"Here he is, your Honor."

"That man? Why, he is armed! Disarm him."

Gonzales handed me his pistol and cartridge-belt with an exceeding bad grace.

"Mr. Gonzales," said Peterson, turning for the first time to the city marshal, "you are here, charged with a very serious offense against the revenue laws of the United States of America. A very serious offense, indeed, sir. It is, of course, impossible for me to give you a hearing now, at two o'clock in the morning, but I can put you under bonds at this time to appear before me later. As your offense is such a serious one, I shall have to fix

the amount of your bail at $20,000. If you are not able to give
that amount of bail, you must pass the night in the military
guard-house at Fort McIntosh."

Poor Gonzales could only stand and stare helplessly at the
Commissioner. He knew Peterson was in earnest, and that he
would do as he said. He also knew he was guilty of smuggling.
Nearly all the Mexicans in Laredo at that time were smugglers.
Peterson had a desk full of affidavits against hundreds of men.
The affidavits were usually made by those having a grudge against
the offenders. Peterson seldom did anything in these cases, but
he carefully kept the affidavits. He thought they might be useful
some time. This was one of the times.

"Mr. Marshal," said Peterson to me, after flooring Gonzales
with the twenty-thousand-dollar-bail proposition, "you will now
go and execute the other *capias*. I will be responsible for this
prisoner until your return."

Taking my posse with me, I went at once to the house of Don
Sixto Navarro. He had gone to bed, and we had some difficulty
in arousing him. When we at last succeeded, and I showed him
the warrant for his arrest he was greatly excited. There was
nothing to do but come with me, however, and he accordingly
dressed himself and came.

At Peterson's office the same action was taken as in the case
of Gonzales. Navarro was told he must give $20,000 bail or go
to the guard-house for the night. He started to protest that the
amount was excessive, but Peterson said he was the best judge
of that, and would not reduce it one cent.

"You may send for bondsmen, if you wish," said the Commissioner, "but you must hurry, as I do not propose to stay up
much longer on this matter."

In ten minutes a dozen Mexicans were scurrying all over the
town, waking up the wealthy men and explaining what was
wanted of them. In half an hour Peterson's office was crowded
with the richest merchants in Laredo. He was exceedingly particular as to who went on the bonds of Gonzales and Navarro,
and it was not until after four o'clock that the prisoners were
allowed to depart. They were to appear for a hearing before
Peterson at ten o'clock that morning. The hour set for our appearance in the court of Magistrate Navarro was nine o'clock.

After the last Mexican had gone, Peterson told me to go to

the door and adjourn court. I did so, and when I turned back to him, he was roaring with laughter.

"I'll turn the old town upside down," he said, as he began to sort over a big quantity of affidavits on his desk. "These affidavits will stir things up. I couldn't convict on them, but I can do a lot of scaring. Some of them are two years old, but I guess they are fresh enough for my purpose."

We lay down and went to sleep then, but arose in time for our appearance in Navarro's court at nine o'clock, and hurried to the office. The little room was crowded to suffocation. The mayor, the sheriff, the county judge, and nearly all the most prominent citizens and merchants were there. Our arrival was the signal for a cessation of the buzz of excited voices and the crowd made way for us to pass.

We took seats near Senor Navarro's desk. That gentleman looked as though he had not slept since we had last seen him. He seemed worried. He cleared his throat nervously and asked in a low tone whether the witnesses against us were present. There was no answer, and the magistrate seemed much relieved thereat. He braced up wonderfully and, smiling at Peterson and me, said pleasantly:

"Gentlemen, you see there are no witnesses against you; I shall have to dismiss the case."

All this had evidently been arranged beforehand, to propitiate the Commissioner, but they little knew the man with whom they had to deal. Peterson merely shrugged his shoulders and asked me to go to breakfast with him. He took not the slightest notice of the numerous greetings of *"Buenos dias, Senor; como esta V.?"* which met his ears continually. We had breakfast in a little restaurant and then went to Peterson's office.

A large crowd had congregated in the street in front of the office, awaiting our arrival. As soon as the office was opened, it was completely filled with men, and many were unable to get in for want of room. I opened court, and Gonzales and Navarro were told to stand up. Peterson looked at them very seriously and then said in a stern voice:

"I am not prepared, right now, to give you a hearing and will put it off in each case for two weeks more. In the meantime, I shall require you to renew your bonds in the sum of twenty thousand dollars each, or you may go to the guard-house, as you please."

Immediately after saying this, the Commissioner turned to me, and in a loud, distinct voice said:

"Mr. Marshal, you will find a number of warrants on my desk. Select those for the mayor, the sheriff, and the most prominent merchants and execute them at once. I propose to put a stop to this smuggling, and the best way to do it is to begin at the top and take the big men first."

This bombshell had an immediate effect. The crowd in the office began to thin out rapidly. The mayor and the sheriff disappeared; so did the prominent merchants. The others were not long in following, and in a few minutes Peterson and I were alone. I was looking over the *capiases* and selecting some of them, according to the Commissioner's instructions, when he said:

"Oh, don't bother with those things. I only wanted to frighten them a little and teach them not to interfere with me."

He had done so very effectually. The accused men went over into Mexico as quickly as they could get there. When Peterson learned of this, he was so tickled that he immediately went on a spree. Then he sent a telegram to the *Galveston News,* of which newspaper he was an occasional correspondent. The telegram read in this way:

"Laredo set on fire. The mayor, sheriff, and big merchants have skipped to Mexico to avoid arrest. Particulars later."

Unfortunately, he was not in a condition to send the later particulars, and so the *Galveston News* came out the next morning with a startling article based on the brief telegram. The headlines of the article read:

LAREDO ON FIRE

TERRIBLE CONFLAGRATION ON THE RIO GRANDE

THE SHERIFF AND MAYOR OF THE CITY SUPPOSED TO BE THE INCENDIARIES

THEY AND THEIR PALS HAVE FLED TO MEXICO

EXCITEMENT ON THE BORDER

Chapter IV

OFF ON A SURVEYING TRIP

Peterson and I left town early the next morning to go on the surveying trip. He was to lay out some homestead sections on the Nueces River, about sixty miles from Laredo. It seemed to me a queer country for anyone to select for a home. The only trees were a few scattered live oaks and mesquite, the latter being utterly useless, except for firewood. Prickly pears grew in abundance. So did rattlesnakes. We were three weeks on the trip. Part of the time I carried a chain and the rest a red flag.

It was hard work and very exciting. The excitement consisted in killing rattlesnakes. We killed, on an average, three snakes to the mile. We saved their rattles, and when we went back to Laredo, Peterson put them in a cuff-box. They completely filled the box. It was on this trip that I learned what a wonderful shot Peterson was with the revolver. One day he killed five "cotton-tail" rabbits without reloading his six-shooter, and he was riding a fractious horse at the time. Never before or since have I seen such marvelous shooting, and in my ten years of far Western life I have met some splendid marksmen.

When we returned to Laredo I continued to act as a deputy United States Marshal. I did not serve any more *capiases* on prominent Mexican citizens, but I did capture some smugglers in the act of bringing dutiable articles across the Rio Grande. I took as "prizes" a cartload of Mexican sugar and three barrels of *mescal*. As there are about five fighting drunks in a quart bottle of *mescal* and subsequently five splitting headaches, my capture was of direct benefit to humanity.

Seizing contraband goods was a precarious way to make a living, however, and I soon saw that I should have to obtain some steadier and more remunerative employment. The unpopularity of the work was another drawback. As seven-tenths of the people were smugglers, either chronic or occasional, I was not exactly a favorite with them. I went to Peterson and resigned.

"How would you like to be on the police force?" he asked.

"We ought to have at least one American on the police here, and, if you want to try it, I will get the appointment from the mayor for you."

I said I would try it, and he sent me with a note to the mayor. Peterson's influence with the authorities since his threat to put a stop to the smuggling would have made a Tammany leader in New York turn pale with envy.

The mayor read the note and at once appointed me chief of police!

To do this he had to depose a Mexican, but he would have turned out his own brother if he had thought he could please Peterson by so doing. I assumed my new duties at once. I hadn't a very clear idea of what they were, but I knew I had them to perform and that there was money to be made in doing it. I received $2.50 from the town for every arrest that I made, and $1 a day was allowed me for every prisoner in the "calaboose," as the jail was called. As it cost me but forty cents a day to board each prisoner, there was a clear profit of sixty cents a day. This system was certainly open to criticism, as it encouraged the policemen in making as many arrests as possible.

I had ten Mexicans under me on the police force. They detested me from the beginning, partly because I had been the cause of the ousting of their former chief, but mainly because I was a "Gringo." The Mexicans on the border called all Americans "Gringos." The Americans retaliated by calling the Mexicans "Greasers." The origin of the term "Gringo" is curious. There is a legend that, in the early days of the Mexican border, a Scotchman made himself unpopular there by overreaching the natives, and it is said that this man was in the constant habit of singing

"Green grow the rushes, O"

The Mexicans couldn't call him "Green grow," but they came as near to it as their tongues could twist the words and called him "Gringo." From that time the nickname gradually became a generic term in speaking of all Americans.

I had not been at the head of the Laredo police force two days before stories of vague threats having been made by some of the policemen under me began to reach my ears. I was young and did not pay much attention to the threats. I reasoned that if the men should become openly hostile I could easily dismiss them from the force. There was no civil-service-reform nonsense about the city government of Laredo.

The third day after my appointment I made my first arrest. The mayor had given me a silver badge, which I put on my coat. I had a .45 calibre six-shooter in a holster, slung to a cartridge-belt about my waist, and I was impressed with the sense of my own dignity and appearance. On this day of my first arrest, I was walking quietly down the street when I saw a Mexican standing on the corner. He was giving a series of wild yells, and as I approached I saw that he was very, very drunk. I went up to him and grasped his arm to lead him to the "calaboose." He looked at me in blank amazement for a moment and then jerked his arm away. Before I could get hold of him again, he reached down to his boot-leg and, drawing a big knife, made a savage pass at me with it, and I retreated a couple of steps. I drew my revolver, cocked it, pointed it at his head and told him to drop the knife and hold up his hands. To my utter astonishment he did nothing of the kind. He backed slowly away.

I did not want to shoot him, nor did I care to get so close to him that he could use his knife on me. I was in a quandary. He backed up to a grocery store and then turned suddenly and ran inside. I ran in after him. There were half a dozen persons in the store, and when they saw me rush in with a revolver in my hand they dodged down behind the counter and boxes and barrels. The man I was after darted out through a rear door.

Before I could follow him, two women ran up to me and threw their arms about my neck. They held tightly to me in this embrace, screaming as loud as they could. I attempted to explain the circumstances to them, but my knowledge of their language was slight, and not at all equal to exciting occasions like this. When I finally did get into their heads the fact that I was a police officer and only wanted to arrest the man for drunkenness, he had disappeared.

I was mad clear through then. I went at once to the policemen on my force, and ordered them to hunt up the drunken man. They did not seem very anxious to obey, but I spoke imperatively and they started out on the search. I took one of them with me, and we began a hunt in that part of the town where I lost the man. We found him late in the afternoon, asleep in a little adobe house belonging to one of his friends. We went in and arrested him and took him to the "calaboose," but he fought like a tiger all the way. The next morning he had to pay a fine of $10.

This incident, although small in itself, led to more important results. The man whom I arrested was a great favorite with his native townsmen, and I did not make a bid for popularity in taking him to jail. One night a week later I was shot at in the street. I heard the bullet whistle by my head and hit the door behind me with a thud. I ran toward the place whence the report of the pistol had come, but could find no one there. The streets were very dark.

Half an hour later I was shot at again. Once more I failed to find the man, who had fled, although I hunted diligently. It was getting very uncomfortable. That night I was shot at five times. I told my policemen about it, and they apparently made great efforts to find the man or men.

There was something in the way they went about it, however, that aroused my suspicions, and I at last came to the conclusion that they were in sympathy with my unknown assailant. Indeed, I was not sure it was not one of my own men who had been firing at me. Be that as it may, I decided I had had enough of chieftainship, and the next day went to the mayor and resigned.

He accepted my resignation without hesitancy. He did not ask me why I resigned, nor did he ask me to remain on the force. I collected something more than twenty dollars for the time I had been chief of police. It did not take me long to spend the money, and once more I found myself without funds or prospect of getting any.

It was at this time that General Porfirio Diaz was leading the revolution in Mexico against the Government under President Sebastian Lerdo. There were several small "battles" in Nueva Laredo, and the inhabitants of Laredo watched them with interest from the bluffs of the Rio Grande on the Texas side. The battles were tame affairs, as viewed from an American standpoint. They were not very bloody, but it was interesting to watch them, and all the inhabitants of Laredo made it a point to go down to the river-front every time firing began on the other side. The river was less than a half a mile wide at that point.

One morning we were awakened by the sound of firing over in Mexico. It began with two or three savage volleys, and continued with a pattering fire, as of raindrops on the dead leaves in a forest. It meant that another battle was in progress, and I dressed as rapidly as I could and hurried down to the banks of the Rio Grande.

Many people were there watching the fight for the possession of the Mexican town. The Lerdists, or Government party, had been in possession of Nueva Laredo for about two weeks, and now the revolutionists were attacking them. Should the revolutionists be victorious and drive the Lerdists from the town, it meant a dead loss to the merchants there. When the Lerdists had captured the place, in accordance with the regular custom of Mexican warfare—on the frontier at least—they had lost no time in levying a *prestamo*. In other words, they forced the merchants to pay them a large sum of money. The revolutionists did the same thing once or twice earlier in the game.

As a matter of fact, both forces on the frontier were composed of unscrupulous bandits who only engaged in the war for the money they could force from the merchants. If the revolutionists won the town again they were certain to make the merchants once more go down into their pockets. There were about two hundred men on a side in this fight. Those in possession of the town had built barricades across the streets. Some of them fought from behind these barricades, and others went to the house-tops and fought from there. On nearly all the flat-roofed houses were raised edges which served admirably for battlements.

The opposing forces had been fighting for about four hours that day, without killing more than two or three men on each side, when it was learned that stray bullets had come over to our side of the river, and wounded two women and killed a boy who was standing in front of his home in Laredo, watching the fight. I reported this to United States Commissioner Peterson, and he sent word to the commanding officer at Fort McIntosh. This officer was Major Henry C. Merriam, later a general in the United States Army.

Major Merriam at once sent a squad of the Twenty-fourth Infantry (colored troops) into Laredo with an old brass muzzle-loading twelve-pounder, the only piece of artillery at the fort. This cannon was placed on a piece of high ground near the bluff which overhung the river.

There it was pointed straight at the Mexican town, half a mile or less away. This proceeding interested the Mexican citizens of Laredo so much that a crowd of them gathered around the colored soldiers and looked at the gun with great curiosity. They had little or nothing to say, but they did not seem pleased. This feeling was so evident, indeed, that all the Americans in the town were quietly supplied with muskets and ammunition from the fort, as a matter of precaution, should it become necessary to proceed to actual hostilities.

Major Merriam would take no further responsibility, however, and said that he would only act under the instructions of the United States Marshal or his deputy. Peterson said that I was the only United States Deputy Marshal in the town and would have to take charge of affairs.

This was interesting for a youth who had only a short time before left the peace and quiet of Philadelphia; but, with a supreme confidence in myself, born of inexperience and tickled vanity, I assumed the responsibility without a protest. But I resolved to take no action without consulting Peterson. How I came to be so modest as that has escaped my memory. By Peterson's advice, I notified a number of men to act as a posse, among them St. Clair and his partner.

With St. Clair, I went down the river bank to the ferry landing and waited for the boat to be punted over from Mexico. By advice of Peterson, I was going to leave St. Clair at the landing with orders to detain any man who should attempt to cross to the other side of the river with arms.

The ferry landing was under the bluff on which the cannon was planted, but a little further down the river. We had hardly reached the place before we heard the "zip" of a bullet as it sped by our heads. In another moment the sound was repeated. Then we heard three or four bullets come humming by us in quick succession. Although perfectly aware of the futility of such action, I could not refrain from ducking my head a little whenever I heard a bullet pass. It is as natural to do that as it is to close one's eye to avoid something flying into it.

"They certainly must be firing at us from across the river," I said to St. Clair; "those can't be accidental shots."

"Right you are, my boy," he answered; "and the quicker we get away from here, the healthier it will be for us."

We looked across the Rio Grande, and two or three more bullets sang by us. One struck in the water in front of us. By this time we had detected a little puff of smoke rising from the bushes that fringed the bluff on the opposite bank. I quickly raised the Winchester rifle borrowed from Peterson, and fired at a point a little under the smoke. A moment later a perfect shower of bullets came by us and we did not linger longer in that vicinity. We didn't exactly run, but we certainly did not waste any time getting away.

But I was glad I fired that shot, and I hoped it did some damage. It tickled me to think that I had fired the first shot from the United States at Mexico, in what I was beginning to imagine would be a war between the two countries. Once more I must remind the reader that I was extraordinarily young and inexperienced in those days.

When we reached the top of the hill where the gun was placed, we found a young lieutenant in charge. His name, I believe, was Glendenning. I told him that we had been fired upon from Mexico, and I added that, in my opinion, a cannon-shot would have a salutary effect about that time.

"Oh, I hardly think it was anything more than a few stray bullets," said the lieutenant.

"I am positive they were firing at us," said I.

"Oh, I don't believe they would do that," said he. "It must have been stray bullets."

Before I could answer him, the familiar sound of the bullets as they hummed by our ears made the officer duck his head and jump for safety behind a little adobe house close by. Arrived at this shelter, he straightened up, threw out his chest, and shouted in a commanding voice:

"Put a shell over that town!"

It was beautiful to see the way those colored soldiers in Uncle Sam's blue uniforms sprang to their positions and made ready to fire the twelve-pounder. They moved like clock-work. Most of the Americans of the town were on the spot by this time, and with the greatest interest they watched the loading and aiming of the gun. Then the gunners fell back a few steps, and the next moment the cannon boomed its defiance to Mexico.

As a shell went screeching over the Rio Grande and burst right above the town of Nueva Laredo, all the Americans gave a loud cheer and flung their hats into the air and shook hands with each other, and laughed and danced for joy. You see, there was no great love, at any time, on that border between the Americans and the Mexicans, and the idea of a fight was soothing and pleasant to the white men there, outnumbered as they were.

The hundred or so of Mexicans who were near the gun did not

cheer or look pleased. They were silent, and seemed very serious.

"Now, men," cried the young lieutenant, "I want you to put a shell or a solid shot over into that town for every bullet that comes this way."

Again the Americans cheered and yelled with pure joy. Foolish? Yes, very, very foolish, but wholly delightful in its patriotism. There were enough Mexicans in those two towns to have massacred every American there, soldiers and all, in fifteen minutes. There were only about thirty soldiers at the fort. Counting every one, there were not more than eighty Americans who could be relied upon in a fight. The Mexican population of the two towns was about five thousand.

But the bullets stopped coming our way. Indeed, the Mexican forces across the Rio Grande were so taken by surprise by the introduction of artillery into their "battle" that they stopped fighting, as though by mutual consent.

There was a sudden clattering of hoofs down the street, and, in a minute, Major Merriam dashed up to the gun on his horse.

"By whose orders did you fire that gun?" he demanded, as the lieutenant saluted.

"Well, sir," said the young officer, "they were firing at us from across the river, and—and this young man, the Deputy Marshal, asked me to fire, so I gave orders to send a shell or a solid shot over there for every bullet that should come this way."

"I told him to fire, sir," I added.

Major Merriam put his hand to his mouth to conceal a smile. Then he said gravely:

"You have done perfectly right, gentlemen. I have just received orders from San Antonio to do exactly what you have done."

Our attention was attracted at this moment to a row-boat which put out from the Mexican bank of the river. Someone in it was holding a white flag and waving it to attract attention. The boat came half way across the river and stopped. Major Merriam studied it for a few minutes with the aid of field-glasses. Then he dismounted and walked down to the river bank, followed by an orderly.

They got into a boat and were rowed out to where the other boat had stopped. There they found the Comandante of the Lerdist, or Government, party. The Comandante demanded to know why his city was bombarded by the United States authorities. Major Merriam told him the reason, and further informed him that if the bullets continued to come over into Laredo he would knock the Mexican town about his ears, or words to that effect.

"If you must fight a battle over there," said Merriam, "you must contrive to do it as they fight on the stage—sideways. It won't do to shoot into the audience."

The boats separated and returned to their respective shores. A quarter of an hour later, the "battle" was raging merrily again, but the combatants seemed to have actually taken the Major's advice and were doing their fighting in such a way as to prevent bullets flying over into Texas.

Now, although this was doubtless highly satisfactory to Major Merriam, it was too tame altogether for the more adventurous spirits among the Americans. The firing of that old cannon had aroused their patriotism and they wanted to hear it boom some more. A few of us consulted together over the situation, and hit upon a plan to have some more fun.

We quietly stole down to a crevice in the bluff on the Texas side of the river, where we could not be seen by the American soldiers. Then we began to fire over into Nueva Laredo. This soon brought a return fire, some of the Mexicans shooting at the gunners on the bluff. In another minute the cannon was roaring again, and this time a solid shot knocked down a little house in the Mexican town. Next, a shell was sent over, and it was quickly followed by a solid shot.

By carefully putting in our rifle-shots where they would do the most good and so drawing a return fire to the cannon, we managed to keep up hostilities all the afternoon, and neither Major Merriam nor the young lieutenant and his soldiers knew that we were the cause of it.

Toward nightfall the revolutionists were driven back from the town of the Lerdists. We learned afterward that their entire loss was two men killed and five wounded! Of course, when they stopped their battle we ceased firing on them and the cannon was silent.

Strange as it may seem, this bombardment of a Mexican town by United States troops did not lead to any international complications. The reason for this probably was that the Mexican Government had its hands full taking care of its domestic troubles. Diaz, as everyone knows, finally succeeded in overthrowing the Government, and on May 5, 1877, became President of the Republic.

One curious incident in connection with the bombardment of the town by the United States soldiers was that the most damage done was to the United States Consul's house in Nueva Laredo. Part of one of the shells tore through his roof, and continued right down through the house to the cellar. Luckily, it did not hit anyone on the way. As the Stars and Stripes were flying from the building at the time, the consul thought the attack on his house was inexcusable. The Mexicans looked upon it as a huge joke.

Chapter V

I JOIN THE MEXICAN REVOLUTIONISTS

The day following the bombardment I quarreled with Peterson. He was intoxicated and in one of his ugly moods, and I was not as indulgent as I might have been, so that we parted on very bad terms. Curiously enough, he did not follow his regular practice and challenge me to mortal combat on the field of honor. I should have peremptorily declined if he had done so. It is as well not to indulge a man in all of his foibles, and one should draw the line when it comes to accepting challenges from fancy pistol-shots.

I was in another bad predicament. Ross and his brother had given up the market-gardening project, and gone back to Atascosa County. I was without money, in a town full of enemies, and knew that as soon as it should be discovered that I had lost the friendship of Peterson my situation would be desperate. There was absolutely no one to whom I could turn, and I wisely concluded that I should have to get out of town. But that was easier determined upon than accomplished. The only way for me to leave the place was to walk. The distance to the nearest town was several days' journey, and I was without provisions or means to procure any.

While I was puzzling what to do, I met a little Irishman named Ryan. He was almost as badly off as I. He hadn't a cent and he wanted to leave Laredo. But he possessed one decided advantage over me—every man in the place was not his enemy. We talked the matter over without coming to any definite conclusion. We did think of applying to the Commissary Sergeant for rations sufficient to last us until we could reach some other settlement, but before we made up our minds to do so we received an offer which promised at least a living.

A Mexican who was in sympathy with the Diaz revolutionists told us he would see that we received a dollar a day if we would go over to Mexico and join the forces outside Nueva Laredo. We were in a desperate mood, and, consequently, accepted his offer without hesitation.

He led us to a point near the Rio Grande, about two miles above Laredo, and left us in an old dugout, in a bluff near the water's edge. He gave us some bread and coffee, and told us to wait there until we heard from him. We waited two days, and, finally, were about to leave the place and go back to Laredo when, on the third afternoon, three men came to our hiding-place. They said they had come to guide us to the revolutionists' camp across the Rio Grande. We followed them, and they led us to where a little boat was hidden farther up the stream. We stepped into it and were poled rapidly over the river. When we reached Mexico, we had to walk about three miles before we came to the revolutionists' camp.

The camp was in the middle of a dense mesquite and cactus chaparral. The revolutionists numbered about three hundred men. It was the most villainous-looking gang I ever had the bad fortune to encounter.

Long association with the "greasers" of the border, which I afterward had, did not tend to elevate my opinion of them as a class, but I never found any quite so bad as that band of revolutionists. They were guerillas of the worst kind. They were thieves, cut-throats, and cowards, and did not possess one redeeming feature, as we very soon discovered. We were not with them two hours before we heartily wished ourselves a hundred miles away.

The man who induced us to join them had told us we were only wanted for our fighting qualities, and that we would have an easy time of it. He said the Mexicans put great store in the fighting qualities of Americans. After having watched the Mexicans in one or two of their "battles," I did not doubt that statement in the least. Those men could shoot oftener in a given space of time without hitting anything than seemed credible. They may have been able to do some fair shooting at a target, but when it came to fighting, their marksmanship was ludicrous. Their one idea seemed to be to pull the trigger as often as possible and trust to luck. I never saw one take aim in a fight.

When we reached the camp we quickly discovered that we could be useful to the revolutionists in other ways than fighting their enemies. We were compelled to go a quarter of a mile for water, to collect wood for the fires, and to do all the heavy work about the camp, while they squatted around blankets and quarreled over *monte*. The revolutionists were abnormally lazy and great gamblers. They all had horses—sorry-looking, ill-fed mustangs; but when we asked for horses they laughed at us. They gave us each a revolver, but there it ended, so far as an outfit was concerned.

For three days we worked from dawn until after dark for those land pirates. We did not get the dollar a day which had been promised to us. We barely got enough to eat.

On the fourth day we were told they were going to make another attack on the town. Then they gave us horses, and pretty bad ones they were. Ryan and I did not feel a bit like helping those fellows to capture the town, but we had no recourse. We started with the troop just before daylight the next morning. When we reached the edge of Nueva Laredo the first faint light showed in the east above the horizon. For some reason, which I was at a loss to understand, we did not at once begin the attack. We waited until the sun was up. Then the order to charge was given, and we started into town pell-mell.

As we went up a long, narrow street, the Lerdists, who were on the house-tops and in many of the windows of the houses, fired on us. Suddenly my horse gave a jump and shot ahead like a racer on the home-stretch. I tried to rein him in, but could not. He had the bit between his teeth, and was going like the wind. Then I saw that he had been shot through the ear.

By the time I discovered what ailed my horse I was far in advance of the revolutionists. I had never led a charge before, and it was not of my own volition that I led this one; but I did it all the same. When I found I was in for it, I ceased trying to hold my horse back. Instead, I urged him to greater exertions. If there was any glory to be won, I thought, I might as well have the credit of trying to win it. So I pulled my revolver, and, yelling in true cowboy fashion, fired at every man I saw.

It was exhilarating and tremendously exciting, and I lost sight of the danger in the fierce fun of the dash up that street. When I reached the market plaza I burst into it with a wild yell and started around it fast as I could go, while rifles blazed from every side. If Americans had been behind those rifles, I should have fallen before I had gone ten yards; but, as it was, I was not touched by a bullet.

I soon saw that the streets leading from the plaza were all

barricaded, with the exception of the one by which I had entered it. I had circled twice around the plaza when the revolutionists reached it and came after me, with a series of blood-curdling yells. Then, on my third round, I darted down the street by which we had entered, and every mother's son of those revolutionists followed me. All were shooting and yelling, and it was exciting to a rare degree. But I had had all I wanted of it for that time, and I went out of the town almost as fast as I entered it.

When we were well clear of the place, I reined in my exhausted pony and waited for the others to come up. They stopped when they reached me, and to my extreme amazement were loud in their praises of what they called my "bravery." I did not think it would be wise to tell them that I led the charge solely because I couldn't help it. If they thought it brave to ride into a town and out again without accomplishing anything, that was strictly their business.

They seemed to think that we had done enough for one day and we rode slowly back to our camp. When we reached it, I thought I would take advantage of my sudden popularity and demand the pay that was due me. I did so, and was told to go and get some water to make coffee. I picked up a bucket and called to Ryan to come with me. As soon as we were out of sight of the camp, I threw down my bucket and told Ryan I was going back to Texas. He followed suit, and we made a bee-line for the Rio Grande. We found a sleepy Mexican in charge of the boat in which we had crossed a few days before. He declined to take us across the river until he should receive orders to do so from the leader of the revolutionists, but we tried the effect of a little moral suasion in the form of two six-shooters held at his head, and he poled us over to the Texas bank with commendable vigor.

Once more on the soil of the United States, we felt that we were safe from pursuit. It was a warm day and we had been up and active very early, so, following the custom of that country, we lay down for a *siesta*. Our couch was the grass-covered prairie and our covering and shelter from the sun's hot rays a mesquite tree.

We slept long, for it was not until the sun's rays were touching the tops of the mesquite trees with a last golden gleam that we awoke. We did not reach Laredo until after dark. I led the way to St. Clair's house. When we arrived there and went in, St. Clair closed the door quickly and bolted it.

"Where do you fellows come from?" he asked.

"Mexico."

"How did you get away from the revolutionists?"

"Walked."

"Desert?"

"Yes."

"I don't blame you. But you shouldn't have come to this town. You were seen attacking the town over there today, and warrants are out for your arrest for filibustering. You'd better light out of this burg as fast as you can travel."

"Give us something to eat first. We can discuss the other afterwards."

St. Clair made some coffee for us and toasted some jerked beef over his fire. Jerked beef might not be highly prized as a delicacy in epicurean circles of the large cities of the North, but as it was served to us that night, it seemed a dainty, fit for a king's table. Our appetites were sharp enough to do it ample justice, and St. Clair, good fellow that he was, seemed delighted to see us empty his larder. We were just finishing the last bit of the supper, when a loud knock came at the door.

"Who's there?" called out St. Clair.

"Open the door instantly," answered a voice which we recognized as belonging to Peterson. "I have come to get two men who were seen to enter your house."

"I'll open my door when I ——— please," cried St. Clair. "There's no one here but myself."

As he said this, he quietly opened a back door and motioned for Ryan and me to go out that way. We did not hesitate long about leaving, but went at once, and found ourselves in a yard surrounded by a high brush fence. As everything that grows in Texas has a more or less wicked thorn, a brush fence in that part of the country is no slight obstacle to surmount, but this was no time to care for a few scratches, so over that thorny fence we scrambled without counting the cost.

We had no sooner reached the further side than we heard a number of men in the yard behind us, and the next moment we saw a bright light back there. It was made by setting fire to a newspaper soaked with kerosene. The light revealed nothing to our pursuers, however, for by that time we were far from the place.

That night we slept in the brush. The next morning we were

both extremely hungry. That may seem curious, after what I have said of the good supper at St. Clair's, but it is a fact that a man is always hungry when he does not know where or how he is to get his next meal. Why this should be I do not know, but anyone who has ever been in such an unenviable predicament will bear me out in my assertion of the fact.

What were we to do? We could not stay out there in the brush and starve to death. We could not go over to Mexico and be shot or hanged for deserting that band of rascally revolutionists. We could not branch out for ourselves and try to walk to another town, for the distance was too great, and we did not know the way. If we went into Laredo we should surely be arrested for filibustering, and stand a good chance of being convicted and sent to prison. We were in a sad quandary, but it was one from which we must speedily extricate ourselves. We discussed the situation in every light and finally, toward the middle of the day, we decided to return to Laredo and face the music. At least, I did; Ryan said he would not return until evening.

I went straight to a restaurant which was kept by an Irishman named McIntyre, and ordered dinner, although I had not a cent to pay for it. I proposed to owe for that meal until I was able to pay for it, with or without the proprietor's permission. I was willing to take the chance of a little unpleasantness with him for the sake of getting a square meal.

Before I had more than half finished my dinner, mine ancient enemy, Gregorio Gonzales, the City Marshal, came in. He was after me and had a *capias* for my arrest. When Peterson quarreled with me he made friends with Gonzales, and appointed him a Deputy United States Marshal.

"Ah," said he, as his eyes fell upon me where I was seated eating my dinner. "I have you at last. I have a warrant for your arrest."

"That's all right," I answered, as I continued to eat.

"You must come right along with me," said Gonzales.

Now I wanted to finish my dinner before going with him, and so I forthwith began to parley for time.

"What do you arrest me for?" I asked.

"For going over into Mexico and fighting with the revolutionists."

"That isn't against the law so long as I didn't go across the river with arms."

"You can explain that to Commissioner Peterson, but I have a warrant for you."

"You say you have, but I haven't seen it. Where is the warrant?"

"Here it is."

"Well, I daresay that is right enough, but you ought to do this thing according to law. You've no right to take me an inch with you until you read that warrant to me. I've been a Deputy Marshal myself, and I know what I'm talking about."

"You can read it yourself," said the Mexican, offering the paper to me.

"Not at all," I answered, with my mouth full; "the law compels you to read it to me. The United States law is very strict about that."

I knew that Gonzales had an extraordinary respect for the forms of the United States laws, and he probably concluded that I was right, and that he had better be on the safe side, for he began to read the paper. He was not much of an English scholar, and he stumbled through the formal document in a way that I enjoyed hugely. It took him a long time to read it. When he got to the end I had finished my dinner. I rose and said that I would go with him. The restaurant proprietor, McIntyre, came forward for his pay.

"Mr. Gonzales will pay you," I said.

Gonzales protested that he would do no such thing.

"That is your affair," I said. "So long as I am your prisoner it is your duty to provide for my wants. Let me go, and I'll pay for the dinner with pleasure; keep me a prisoner, and you'll have to pay for it yourself."

"That's right," put in McIntyre.

With a very bad grace my captor paid the bill, and we left the restaurant.

We went straight to Peterson's office. The Commissioner was very gracious in his manner toward me, but said that he would have to put me under $5,000 bonds to answer for crossing the Rio Grande to Mexico with arms and fighting against the Mexican Government, in violation of the neutrality laws. He asked me if I thought I could get a bondsman, and I said it was not at all likely. I asked permission to write some letters at his desk, and he granted it with much courtesy. He seemed to be sorry to see me in such trouble.

While I was writing Ryan was brought in. He had been arrested as he was entering the town, having decided not to wait until evening before coming in. He was told that he would have to give $2,500 bail. Why my bail was fixed at double the amount of his I did not inquire. Ryan was no more able than I to get a bondsman, and we had a forlorn prospect before us. Peterson said he would give us until six o'clock to get bail; after that hour we should have to go to the guard-house at Fort McIntosh. Ryan and I sat in the office talking it all over, and wondering what the result would be. He wasn't as philosophical as I—he hadn't eaten a dinner—but neither of us expected much less than four or five years in a military prison.

As we sat talking, I happened to look out of the open door, and in doing so I saw a man whom I had met in Atascosa County. His name was Crockett Kelly, and he owned a little ranch near that of John Ross. Kelly was a superb-looking man and a frontier dandy at that time. He was tall and finely proportioned. His face was strong and handsome. His eye was as keen as an eagle's; his hair was black, and fell in long curls over his shoulders. He looked the border hero of romance, and he became a real hero for me that day. I hadn't known him very intimately in Atascosa County, but we had been fishing together a number of times and were good friends. The minute I saw him through Peterson's doorway, I felt that he would in some manner help me. I went to the door and called him. He came at once across the street and greeted me heartily. I told him what trouble I was in. He listened gravely, and when I had finished, said:

"I think I can help you, my boy. How much did you say was your bail?"

"Five thousand dollars, and Ryan's is twenty-five hundred."

"Well, it seems to me that is a little steep, but if the Commissioner will take me I'll go on a bond for both of you. I know you are not going to run away, and something may turn up in a day or two to get you out of the scrape."

Peterson consented to take Kelly as our bondsman, although I was positive Kelly was not worth anything like the amount of our bail. How he satisfied Peterson he was good for it I did not care to inquire. I did ask, however, who had made the affidavit against us upon which we were arrested. Peterson showed the affidavit. It was signed by the man I had arrested for being drunk and yelling on the streets when I was chief of police. In the affidavit he stated that he had seen us crossing the Rio Grande with arms. This was not true; we had been supplied with arms when we reached the revolutionists' camp, not before.

That evening we went with Kelly to the house of the man who made the affidavit. We found him in and accused him of perjury. He denied it. We had a stormy interview, which was only brought to a close by our making him sign a statement to the effect that his affidavit was a series of lies from beginning to end. I wrote out his retraction and he signed it with a six-shooter held to his head while he wrote. This may seem to have been a high-handed way of getting what we wanted, but in that country, and in those days, it was not such a peculiar manner of doing business. The Revolver was King of the Texas frontier then.

Peterson accepted the retraction, the next morning, as a withdrawal of the charges against us. We had no hesitancy in telling him how we obtained it, but the irregularity of our method only amused him. He tore up the papers and declared there was no case against us. When I think it all over, I feel confident the Commissioner never seriously intended to push the case, but was merely playing one of his practical jokes on us.

When I visited Laredo in 1892, I learned that Peterson had long been dead.

Chapter VI

Once again I was confronted with the problem of how to get away from Laredo, and its solution was as difficult as ever. The more I thought it over, the more desperate did the predicament seem. I should have liked to go with Kelly, but, unfortunately, that was not possible, he being on his way on horseback to Camargo, in Mexico. Even if I had a horse I should not have cared to risk going into Mexico after my experience there. Ryan had obtained employment as a waiter in McIntyre's little restaurant, but I had exhausted all my chances to make a living in the town and my only recourse was to leave it.

But how? The prospect of walking scores of miles over that desolate Rio Grande country, alone, depending for maintenance upon what I could get at the widely scattered ranches, was not an enticing one, but I realized that I should have to come to it sooner or later, and the quicker I got away from my enemies the better it would be for me.

I was standing on a corner one morning, trying to make up my mind to start on my perilous and lonely journey, when, looking up the street, I saw a troop of horsemen coming toward me. As they approached, I saw that they were Americans, and for a moment I thought they were cow-boys. But what, I asked myself, were so many cow-boys doing together? I counted them as they rode by; there were forty-two of them.

And at their head rode a man who was surely not a cow-boy, whatever the others might be. This leader was rather under the average height and slimly built, but he sat so erect in the saddle and had such an air of command that he seemed like a cavalry officer at the head of a company of soldiers.

But it was easy to see these men were not soldiers. They were heavily armed, to be sure, but they wore no uniforms, and were nearly all beardless youths. The leader himself seemed not more than thirty years of age, although he wore a heavy dark brown mustache and "goatee," which, at a first glance, made him look slightly older.

I was still wondering what manner of men these were, when I saw the leader suddenly hold up his hand and, at the signal, the troop halted. The leader spoke a few words to one who rode directly behind him; then he turned down a side street and galloped away. The one to whom he had spoken gave the order, "Forward, march!" and in another minute the troop had trotted far down the street and out of the town. Then I asked a Mexican who was standing near me if he knew what horsemen those were. He answered in English:

"Why, those are McNelly's Rangers. They're on their way down the river."

I needed no further explanation. Many times had I heard of the Texas Rangers since I had been in the State, and marvelous were the tales which had come to my ears concerning their reckless courage and wonderful riding. They were the mounted frontier police force of Texas and were noted for their deeds of daring all over the West. I had pictured them as bearded ruffians (going about with bowie-knives in their teeth, I had believed), but here they were, a lot of boys of my own age, and led by a captain not much older. I was interested.

"Where are they going from here?" I asked.

"No man can tell that," answered my informant; "but I have heard that they were expected down around Brownsville, and for that reason I said they were going down the river, but they may be just as likely going up the river. No one ever knows where they will turn up. I think they have gone into camp now, just outside the town. I know that Captain McNelly has gone to the hotel with his wife and daughter and son."

I thanked the Mexican for his information and walked slowly away, turning over in my mind a new idea which he had unwittingly put into it.

Why shouldn't I join the Rangers? Here was a chance to get out of Laredo and to gratify my love for adventure at the same time. The men in the troops were of my own age. I was strong, and a fairly good rider. I had seen some little service under fire in the last week or so, and I was willing to see more in the company of my own countrymen. I resolved to apply at once to Captain McNelly for a place in his troop. I went straight to the little hotel where he was said to be stopping and inquired for him. He sent word for me to come to his room.

I found him sitting by the window, talking to his sweet-faced wife. A little girl of about twelve years and a boy of about ten were near them. My experience in Laredo in the last few weeks had not tended to add to the attractiveness of my appearance. I had not been shaved for two weeks and my clothing was almost ragged. I wore a brown handkerchief knotted around my neck in lieu of a cravat, my legs were encased in high and rather shabby boots, and I carried in my hand a *sombrero* which was somewhat the worse for hard usage—I had been using it, doubled up, as a pillow in the brush. I was not prepared to meet a lady and her presence embarrassed me, but my business was with the captain and I did not hesitate to state it plainly.

"I have come, sir," I said, "to ask you to take me into your Rangers. I must apologize for my rough appearance, but I have had a hard experience in this country lately and been without money to buy food, let alone clothes. I should like very much to join the Rangers, and if you'll take me, I believe I can give you satisfaction."

"H'm—what's your name?" the captain asked as he looked searchingly at me with his keen blue eyes.

I told him.

"You are from the North?"

"I am a Philadelphian, sir."

"That's a long distance from here. What brought you into this country?"

"I came here to try to make a little money and to see some wild life and adventure."

"Well, you look as if you'd been doing the latter, anyhow. If you join my troop you'll see all the adventure you want. Can you ride?"

"I can."

"Very well. Come back to me at three o'clock this afternoon, and I'll tell you what I can do for you."

This was not discouraging, for I thought if he had not had some idea of taking me he would have said so at once. I determined to be on hand promptly at the hour he named. I wandered aimlessly about town for an hour or so. After awhile I met St. Clair

"Hello!" he exclaimed. "I've been looking for you. I saw Cap

McNelly, of the Rangers, a little while ago. He's an old friend of mine. He asked me about you and I cracked you up all I knew how. I told him you went over to Mexico and led the revolutionists in a charge on the town over there, just for the fun of the thing, and it seemed to tickle him. That's the kind of stuff he likes. I think he'll take you in his company."

This was good news for me, and, as it was near the appointed hour, I went to the little hotel. The Captain was standing in the doorway.

"I have decided to let you join," were his first words. "You'll have to get a horse, saddle and bridle, a couple of blankets and a six-shooter. The State furnishes your carbine. You'd better ride out to our camp this evening, as we are going away early in the morning."

Then he turned and went into the hotel. If he had waited to note the effect of his words, he probably would have been astonished, for I must have looked the picture of despair. If he had told me that the entrance-fee to his troop was ten thousand dollars in gold, it would not have staggered me more than what he said about the horse, saddle, bridle and blankets, and, it seemed to me, the money would have been as easy to obtain at that time. I was completely disheartened, and walked slowly away from the hotel, in a desperate mood.

I wandered up the street and entered a store kept by an American. I had no object in going into the store, except, perhaps, to pass away the time with the proprietor, who had always been rather friendly to me. I told him of my hard luck in having a chance to join the Rangers and how my hopes were suddenly extinguished by the insurmountable obstacle of being obliged to provide the horse and accoutrements. He sympathized with me, but could offer no suggestion to help me out of my trouble. I was about to leave when a voice called out from the other side of a canvas-wall at the end of the store:

"Come in here and see me, and maybe I can help you out of your fix."

I recognized the voice. It was that of one of the mounted inspectors of customs who patroled the banks of the Rio Grande, a young man named Burbank. He lived in a room partitioned off from the store by the canvas-wall. I had met him only casually, and knew nothing about him except that he was a remarkably

A TEXAS RANGER

fine billiard player. I went directly into his room when he called
me, and found him lounging on the bed, smoking a cigarette.

"You seem to be in tough luck," he said as I entered. "I've
had my eye on you lately, and I know you'll have to get out of
Laredo pretty quick or you'll be carried out feet first. I'll get you
a horse and whatever else you need, and you may give me an
order on Captain McNelly for the amount. He can deduct it
from your pay."

I started to express my gratitude, but he interrupted me and
said:

"That's all right; don't say a word. I'm willing to help a fellow
when I can, and this is only putting out a little money I have no
immediate use for. Next time you see a chap in a hard fix, you
try and help him out; that's the best way to show gratitude."

Burbank went with me to see Captain McNelly. The Captain
said he would accept the order on my pay and give Burbank $10
a month until the amount was all paid. Then Burbank and I went
and bought a horse. He was a light gray, and as pretty a pony as
we could find. He cost $30, a high price for a horse in that coun-
try at the time. Within an hour I had everything I needed, and
a very fine outfit it was. Burbank treated me to a farewell supper
at the restaurant. It was the first meal I had eaten since the preceding day. After supper I mounted my horse, shook hands with
my benefactor, and rode out to the Ranger camp. I was more
than happy to leave the town, for I had undergone much misery
there and hoped never to see the place again.

It was only about two miles from the town to where the Rangers were camped for the night. It was dark, however, when I
started from the restaurant and so the first intimation that I had
reached the camp was a voice calling to me through the gloom:

"Halt!"

So sudden and unexpected was this order that it made me pull
my horse back on his haunches.

"Who goes there?" came the quick demand.

"A friend," I answered.

"Dismount, friend, advance and be recognized."

I threw my leg over the saddle to dismount, but as I did so my
horse started violently and dragged me forward with one of my
feet in the stirrup and the other hopping along the ground. I was
pulled along thus for at least thirty feet before I managed to stop
my horse.

"Hi! hold up! What in —— are you doing?" yelled a man, who jumped from the ground where he had been lying. "Do you want to run over me?"

I extricated my foot from the stirrup and explained that my horse had started with me just as I was dismounting and had dragged me over the ground.

"He must have been ridden by a Greaser," commented the man whom I had so suddenly aroused. "They have a playful habit of giving a horse a cut with the quirt when they get off him, and he learns to expect this and tries to get out of the way. But who are you, anyway, and what are you doing here?"

"That's what I want to know," put in another young man, who stood by with a carbine in his hands. "I told you to advance and be recognized, but I didn't look for you to come on in such a devil of a hurry. Who are you?"

"I'm a new recruit," I answered. "Captain McNelly sent me out here to join."

"Well, if that's so, I'm glad to see you," said the man with the carbine. "Shake. My name's McKinney—Charles McKinney. This man you tried to kill with that horse of yours just now is Evans, but he's such a big, ungainly brute we call him 'Lumber.'"

"Thanks, Girlie, for the introduction," said Evans, or "Lumber," as he was always known in the troop. "You musn't mind what she says," he added as he turned to me. "She's young and foolish. But if you've come to stay, pull off your saddle and make yourself at home. Girlie will stake out your horse for you, seeing it's your first night. Had your supper? Good. Well, spread your blankets and turn in; we're going to make an early start in the morning."

While he was talking and I taking the saddle off my horse, I had an opportunity to observe both young men. As they turned out to be my closest friends in the Rangers for the next three years, I might as well take this opportunity to describe them.

Tom Evans was a native Texan, and, by the way, almost the only one in the troop. He was a giant in stature, and as strong as a mustang. Like nearly all very large men, he was exceedingly good-natured and had one of the happiest of dispositions. It took a great deal to arouse him to anger, but when once provoked beyond endurance, he was a man to be feared. He was exasperatingly lazy, and it was his habit to sprawl at full length on the ground whenever opportunity offered. This and his great size and clumsiness were what gained for him the nickname of "Lumber." When I first knew him, he was but nineteen years old, and had left school, in Austin, only about a year before. Like nearly all in the troop, he had joined the Rangers from pure love of adventure and excitement. He always said that he was destined, sooner or later, to be shot in the abdomen—only he didn't express it exactly that way. Lumber certainly offered a superb target in that portion of his anatomy for stray bullets.

Charley McKinney was the direct opposite of Evans in every way. He was small and wiry, and as active as a wildcat. He had the prettiest pink-and-white complexion, the mildest and softest blue eyes, golden hair, which curled in little ringlets all over his head; a Cupid's bow of a mouth, and an expression of feminine innocence—except when he was on the warpath. The boys had nicknamed him "Girlie," which annoyed him exceedingly, although he strove not to show that he minded it. He was a general favorite, for he was of a lively, generous disposition, had a quick wit, could tell a good story and sing a jolly song, and, with it all, he was as fearless a daredevil as ever reached the Texas frontier. The man who attempted to impose upon Charley McKinney because of his innocent appearance invariably regretted it.

These two men were the first of the troop I met, and they at this day conjure up fond memories, although of all of my old comrades in the Texas Rangers I have the most kindly recollections. Further on, I shall take up the troop in detail and show just what manner of men composed it.

Within fifteen minutes after I rode into the camp, I lay down on my blankets spread out on the ground and, using my saddle for a pillow, soon dropped asleep. For the first time in many nights I felt safe and free from care or worry, and slept well.

Chapter VII

The first faint glimmering of dawn was lighting the sky in the east when I awoke the next morning. The awakening was peculiar. It began with a confused dream, in which I thought myself in a church where all the congregation were singing the hymn, "There's one wide river, and that wide river is Jordan." I remember that I looked about me and recognized many persons whom I had often seen in the church which I attended in Philadelphia, only, instead of being in that church, I was in a little backwoods Sunday-school in the mountains of East Tennessee. The singing grew louder and louder, and at last I awoke with a start. Even then it did not cease, but assailed my waking senses with renewed vigor. I sat up and found myself surrounded by fifteen or twenty Rangers, all of them looking at me and singing about the "one wide river" as loud as they could howl.

It surprised me not a little to see those wild and reckless border riders beginning the day so devoutly, and I looked at them in blank amazement. This seemed to stimulate them to greater exertions, for they not only continued to sing, but presently began to dance with a slow, measured step, as though they were performing some strange religious rite. They joined hands as they danced and circled around me. Gradually, they increased their speed until, in the end, they were all whirling about me in a bewildering, dizzy ring, like so many madmen.

Of a sudden they stopped and gave a series of wild, blood-curdling yells, such as are never heard save in the far West. There, the men on the great silent plains feel sometimes that they must let out their voices with all their power, just to break the monotony of that stillness which is one of the most impressive features of a seemingly limitless prairie. Having thus given vent to their feelings in the early morning, the Rangers started off in various directions to attend to their horses and prepare breakfast, leaving me to recover from my astonishment and confusion at my leisure.

"Did the boys wake you up?" asked a voice close to me.

I looked around and saw McKinney regarding me with a grin.

"Oh, no," I answered facetiously; "they soothed me to sleep. Do they always start the day that way?"

"Not unless there's a stranger in camp," he said. "Then they do it to break the ice of reserve which might otherwise congeal about him."

"Thanks for the explanation. The ice is well cracked in my case."

"Then you'd better go and give your horse some corn. You'll find a sack of corn in the wagon. I wouldn't give him more than two quarts. After you've done that, come back and take breakfast at my dab."

"At your what?"

"Dab."

"What's a dab?"

"Oh, I forgot; of course you couldn't be expected to know. We call the messes 'dabs,' in this outfit. There are only four men in our dab at present and we can easily accommodate another. If you want to join it you're welcome."

I thanked him and told him nothing would give me greater pleasure than to make the fifth man at his dab. Then I went and attended to my horse. When I returned, I pitched in and helped to prepare breakfast. It was like any other camp breakfast in that country: bread, cooked in a skillet, or Dutch oven; beefsteak, fried; and coffee. The last was so strong that it was quite black. It was made by putting a pint cupful of ground coffee-beans into a two-quart coffee-pot, and boiling for half an hour. That coffee would have eaten a hole in a piece of plate glass if it had been given time, but everyone drank a big cupful of it, without milk, and enjoyed it hugely.

It used to be said in Texas that the only way to find out whether coffee was strong enough to drink was to put an iron wedge into the coffee-pot. If the wedge floated, the coffee was sufficiently strong.

We didn't try the test that morning—it wasn't necessary.

As soon as we had eaten breakfast, all the cooking utensils were packed into a box and put into one of the two wagons which were in the camp and which constituted our wagon-train. Then the order came to saddle our horses. As soon as this was done, a very young man with a little dark down on his upper lip, in lieu of a mustache, mounted his horse and called out:

"Fall in!"

Instantly every man swung himself into his saddle and began to form part of a long line in "company-front." The young man rode up in front of the line and said:

"Right dress!"

The line became straighter.

"Count off from right to left."

It was done.

"Count off by twos."

The men counted as directed.

"Twos right, right forward—march!"

As he pronounced the last word, he started off and the troop followed after him in double file. I found myself riding by the side of Charley McKinney.

"Where are we going?" I asked him.

"*Quien sabe?*" he answered. "We never know where we're going until we get there."

Nearly everyone has heard of the Texas Rangers at some time in his life, but how many know what the Rangers really are, or what are their duties? In a general way, everyone knows they are men who ride around on the Texas border, do a good deal of shooting, and now and then get killed or kill someone. But why they ride around, or why they do the shooting, is a question which might go begging for an answer for a long time without getting a correct one.

At the period of which I write, there were six Ranger troops in Texas. Five of these went to form what was known as the Frontier Battalion, which, at that time, was commanded by Major Jones, a very efficient and brave officer. Jones' battalion was mainly engaged on the upper frontier—near the New Mexico line—against Indian invasion. One or two of the troops in the battalion ranged over the southern edge of the Staked Plains, in the "Pan Handle" of Texas; the others did most of their work along the Rio Grande, in the neighborhood of El Paso del Norte.

In addition to the battalion, Captain L. H. McNelly had organized an independent troop of Rangers. They were known officially as "Company A, Frontiersmen."

This was the troop I joined.

The duties of McNelly's troop were very different from those of the other Rangers. To McNelly's men was assigned the work of protecting the Texas side of the lower Rio Grande from the invasion of Mexican cattle-thieves and horse-thieves, but these Rangers also had roving commissions which gave them power to make arrests in any part of the State west of the Colorado River. Each man had virtually the authority of a sheriff, and even more, for the Rangers were not hampered by county boundaries.

At that time, the Texas desperado was in the height of his glory. Large bands of these outlaws were organized all through Western Texas, and the honest, hard-working frontiersmen were completely under their rule. The sheriffs were wholly unable to cope with them. Indeed, in a number of counties the desperadoes were in such numbers and held such power that they were able to elect one of their own number to the office of sheriff. In one county they not only elected the sheriff, but also put in their own men as county judges, justices of the peace, and minor county officials.

The United States troops were on the frontier in large numbers, but they were unable to subdue the Mexican and white desperadoes. This was not the fault so much of the soldiers as it was of the military red tape by which they were bound. The cavalrymen had to be careful not to ride their horses to death in pursuit, and that alone was a sufficient reason for the ease with which the desperadoes eluded them.

Along the lower Rio Grande much cattle and horse stealing was continually going on. Bands of Mexicans, often under the leadership of some white outlaw, made frequent raids from Mexico into Texas and, gathering together all the cattle and horses they could handle, drove them back into Mexico. These men worked so systematically and were so perfectly organized that they successfully defied or eluded all attempts to bring them to justice. They laughed at the abortive attempts of the United States cavalry to catch them. They could not only outride the cavalry—for the reason I have stated—but they could always escape across the Rio Grande when they were close pressed, for beyond that barrier the soldiers of Uncle Sam could not follow them for fear of international complications.

The people living across the border, who had been harassed so long by these marauders, made application to the State Legislature for relief and protection. It was decided to put a troop of Rangers in the field. Captain McNelly, whose fame and daring as an officer in the Confederate service, and later in the Texas State Police during reconstruction days under Governor Davis, had spread from Louisiana to New Mexico, was put in command. There was quite a fight in the Legislature over the bill creating McNelly's troop, the legislators from the eastern portion of the State opposing it as unnecessary. They said that the sheriffs should be able to cope with any lawless persons in Western Texas, as they were in Eastern Texas. Finally the objectors consented to support the bill only upon the condition that a clause be inserted confining the Rangers' operations to the country west of the Colorado River. No other authority than that of the sheriffs was needed east of that stream, they said.

There came a time, it may be remarked, when those wise men had occasion to regret the insertion of that clause, for the desperadoes took advantage of it and sought refuge in the eastern part of the State after we had driven them from the west.

As I have said, much individual power was given to the members of McNelly's troop. Any member could summon all the citizens he wished as a *posse comitatus* to assist him in making arrests, but this was a privilege of which the Rangers seldom took advantage. Indeed, I do not remember ever to have known of an instance where outsiders were called upon to assist in making arrests, although occasionally their services were enlisted as guides to some desperado camp or stronghold.

There was one practice of the Rangers which undoubtedly added much to their success in ridding the community of evildoers—they almost invariably arrested men without warrants. The Rangers had no legal right to do this, but the condition of the country made it a sensible thing to do. Of course, if warrants were given to the men to execute, they did so, but even in such cases they usually had the papers tucked away in an inside pocket and did not display them in making the arrests.

When a Ranger wanted to arrest a man his first action was to draw his six-shooter and "get the drop" on his prospective prisoner. It was a simple matter to take him into custody after that, for no matter how desperate a man might be, he would not take the chances of resisting arrest when he was looking into the muzzle of a loaded revolver with a Ranger's finger playing nervously around the trigger thereof.

I heard of but one man who would not give up when a Ranger "had the drop" on him. That particular desperado had sworn that he would rather die than submit to arrest, and he kept his oath. He did die, but not before he had managed to fire his revolver three times at the two Rangers who were after him.

The Rangers (privates) received $40 a month and rations. The State supplied carbines and ammunition, but the men could choose any style of arms they preferred. Winchesters or Sharp's carbines were the favorite guns, and Colt's or Smith & Wesson's large calibre six-shooters were used exclusively for small-arms. The Rangers supplied their own six-shooters as a matter of course; for each man who joined the command owned and carried a revolver just as everyone did in Texas in the '70's. Two or three of the men had fine breech-loading shotguns—very effective weapons at close quarters with nine buckshot to the barrel. Nearly every man carried a bowie-knife, but that was more for use in and about camp than for offensive or defensive purposes.

The men had to supply their own horses and saddles, but if a horse was killed or used up in the service of the State, the State paid for it—and paid a rattling good price, too. I never heard of the State paying less than $100 for a dead horse, and I never knew a Ranger to pay more than $40 for a live one. As a rule, $20 to $30 was the price paid. The difference between what the State paid and what the Ranger paid was, of course, pure profit to the Ranger. I do not believe such was the understanding in the Adjutant-General's office, but I never heard of anyone taking pains to inquire very closely into the matter.

Chapter VIII

PERSONAL HISTORY OF THE OFFICERS AND MEN OF MC NELLY'S TROOP

Having given some idea of what the Rangers were and what were their duties, I shall, before going into a detailed description of the fights and adventures of the troop, proceed to tell something of the personal history and character of the men and officers composing it.

Our Captain, L. H. McNelly, was well fitted for the work he had to do. For nearly fifteen years he had lived in the saddle, and had done more than his share of hard riding and fighting in the war and during the troublous reconstruction times. From a number of old comrades of McNelly, notably Mr. W. A. Kerr, of Encinal, Texas, who served in the Confederate army with him, I have gathered the following incidents of his career.

McNelly was only seventeen years old when the war between the North and South broke out. He was engaged at that time in herding sheep for T. J. Burton, a sheep man, of Washington County, Texas. Captain George Campbell raised a company in the county to join Colonel Tom Green's regiment, Sibley's brigade, at San Antonio. Young McNelly wanted very much to go to the front, but was such a boy that he found it difficult to persuade Captain Campbell to accept him. He at last did so, however, and so became a duly enlisted private in Company F, Fifth Regiment, Texas Mounted Volunteers, C. S. A.

The first engagement McNelly was in was at Valverde, Mexico, just across the Rio Grande. Colonel Green was in command of the entire Confederate forces there and Captain Joe Sayers commanded the Confederate battery of light artillery. Captain Sayers was anxious to find out the exact position of the Federal forces, so that he could turn his battery loose on them, and Green also wished to know their disposition. Young McNelly volunteered to try and get the information, and all day long was on horseback with a few men, pressing the Federal pickets back in order to locate the forces.

Between the lines was open country, and McNelly was in plain view from both sides. He rode all day, thus exposed, amid a storm of bullets. In his shirt was a book he had been reading, and a bullet hit this book and tore it to pieces, but McNelly was unhurt. He did very valuable service, and when the charge was ordered he was in the front and the first of all to reach the Federal battery. The Union forces retreated across the Rio Grande and McNelly led in the pursuit.

Colonel Green commended the young soldier very highly for his good work and made him an aide on his staff. When Green returned to Texas, he took his regiment to Galveston and captured the Union forces there. McNelly was on the cotton-boat which captured the Harriet Lane, and was the first Confederate to board the Union boat. Colonel Green was promoted to a Generalship and took his command in Louisiana, and it was there that McNelly did his best work for the Confederacy. He was commissioned to raise a scouting company and he gathered about him a troop of reckless young riders and fighters. His dash and courage became proverbial and his exploits were the theme of many a camp-fire story.

At one time he was scouting between Brashear City and New Orleans, after the forces under General Green had captured the former place. The young Captain had been sent about four miles from the main command to scout along the railroad. He discovered a large force of Federals in the woods. McNelly had about forty men, and he found that the Federals numbered about eight hundred, together with nearly two thousand negroes who had flocked to them from the plantations.

There was a long bridge about a quarter of a mile from the Union men. McNelly waited until night and then started his men running back and forth over the bridge, at the same time shouting commands for colonels and generals to move up on the right and left. His men kept galloping and trotting over that bridge for an hour, and by that time the Union men were sure all the Rebs in the country were on them. Then McNelly took his forty men with him, at daylight, with a flag of truce to the Federal camp and demanded an unconditional surrender. The Union officer was sure he was surrounded by a greatly superior force and was glad to surrender.

McNelly and his forty men led the eight hundred prisoners to the Confederate lines, four miles off, and delivered them to

General Green. After that exploit McNelly, with his picked men of the brigade, harassed the enemy under General Banks continually. McNelly went into Fort Hudson as a spy for General Green and obtained valuable information which was used to advantage in capturing the fort afterward.

He was a thin, pale-faced youth, but was very athletic. On one or two of his spying expeditions he was disguised as a woman. During the last eighteen months of the war he had a hundred picked men under him and they did superb scouting work. The Union men called McNelly's scouts guerillas. McNelly's command, his old comrades say, took more prisoners and killed more men than any regiment in Louisiana. Most of their work was done inside the Federal lines and they had a fight about every day, generally in the Louisiana swamps.

In 1870 Governor E. J. Davis, of Texas, asked McNelly to take command of the State Police. McNelly went to see Governor Davis and said to him:

"I'm a Democrat, Governor, and you are a Republican."

"Yes, I know that," said Governor Davis, "but I'm not looking for a politician, sir; I'm hunting a soldier and a brave man for the place. My experience with you on the Mississippi, when I was in command at Morganza and you were on the other side, enables me to know you're the man I want. You know how I am regarded by all who were in your army. You were there and you possibly may be able to mollify some of my enemies in the State."

McNelly consulted General Shelby and Buck Walton, Davis' most bitter opponents, and they advised McNelly to take the place offered him. He did so and rendered great service to the State, although he never succeeded in making either his police or Governor Davis popular in Texas.

McNelly was wounded but once during the war, but he had countless narrow escapes. He was literally the hero of a hundred battles and skirmishes.

When I knew him in the Rangers, he was a very quiet, reserved, sedate sort of a man, but he always had a pleasant word for those under him and was greatly loved by all the men. I was his field-secretary for a time and was brought much into personal touch with him, and I never saw him lose his temper or heard him raise his voice in anger. Although the life of the Rangers was exciting enough for the rest of us, it seemed tame, apparently, to our Captain after his war experiences. I saw him in a number of tight places, as will appear later on, and a more cool and collected individual under fire it would be impossible to imagine.

Such was our leader, and it may be believed that with his experience his choice of men to serve under him was excellent.

For the benefit of my old comrades in the Rangers who are still alive and who may find some little pleasure in the perusal of these pages, I here give the roster of the old troop:

Captain L. H. McNelly,* First Lieutenant L. B. Wright,* Second Lieutenant T. J. Robinson,* First Sergeant R. P. Orrell, Sergeant Linton L. Wright,* Sergeant J. B. Armstrong, Sergeant George Hall,* Corporals M. C. Williams, and W. L. Rudd, Privates S. J. Adams, "Black" Allen, George Boyd, Thomas Deggs, L. P. Durham, T. N. Divine, Thomas J. Evans, M. Fleming, ——Griffen, B. Gorman, Andy Gourley, Nelson Gregory, S. N. Hardy, N. A. Jennings, Horace Maben, A. S. Mackey, Thomas McGovern, John McNelly, Thomas Melvin, Edward Mayers, "Cow" McKay, Charles B. McKinney,* W. W. McKinney, S. M. Nichols, A. L. Parrott, T. M. Quensberry, Jack Racy, H. J. Rector, W. O. Reichel, Horace Rowe, Jesus Sandoval,* G. M. Scott, F. Siebert, L. S. Smith,* D. R. Smith,* S. W. Stanley, N. R. Stegall, T. J. Sullivan, G. W. Talley,* Alfred Walker, W. T. Welsh, James Williams, R. H. Wells, David Watson, F. J. Williams.

In the foregoing list I have marked those whom I know to have died, but, as a matter of fact, not more than a quarter of the old troop are living at this date, 1898.

Jesse Lee Hall, who at the death of Captain McNelly succeeded to the command of the troop, joined it as Second Lieutenant, August 1, 1876, at Oakville. He left the service in 1880 and was succeeded by Captain Ogilsbie. Hall was a famous Ranger captain, and I shall have much to say of his exploits later on.

L. B. Wright left the service in 1876 and became a practicing physician at San Diego, Texas. His brother, L. L. Wright, became Sheriff of Duval County, of which San Diego is the county seat. Both brothers died in the fall of 1892, in the same week. Just prior to their death, they furnished me with notes and recollections of their Ranger experiences and I have used them freely in the following pages.

Lieutenant Robinson was killed in a duel in Virginia, his home.

*Deceased.

He resigned his commission for the sole purpose of fighting that duel. He killed his man and was killed at the same instant. The duel was occasioned by an insult to Robinson's sister in Virginia.

Charley McKinney was murdered in 1890, while attempting to arrest an outlaw. McKinney at the time was Sheriff of La Salle County. His murderer was afterward hanged at San Antonio.

I wish to express here my indebtedness for much material used in his book to Captain Hall, Major Armstrong, Hon. T. N. Divine, John McNelly, and Edward Mayers, who kindly assisted me in gathering together the details of half-forgotten Ranger history during my visit to Texas, a few years ago.

As soon as the bill constituting the Ranger troop passed the Legislature and received the Governor's signature, Captain McNelly began to raise his company. He had thousands of applications from men who wanted to serve under him, but he was very particular in his selection of them. He would take only young men who were educated, of good character, and of a lively disposition. Then, too, the applicants had to convince the Captain that they possessed courage and were good riders, but the latter qualification was a common one in Texas. Although McNelly was himself a Texan, he was seemingly careful to exclude Texans from his troop and, with the exception of Evans, the McKinney boys, and one or two more, he had none. He reasoned that Texans might have friends or "kinfolk" among the very men he would have to hunt down, and he knew how important it was that he should be able to place absolute reliance in each individual member of the troop. The consequence was that it was made up of young men from nearly every Southern State. I was the only member whose home was north of Mason and Dixon's line. There were a number of Virginians; Georgia supplied a good quota; so did Mississippi; so did Alabama. There was one Scotchman (McKay), one Irishman (McGovern), and one Englishman (Rudd). Rudd was a little bit of a red-headed and red-faced Londoner, who always rode the biggest horse in the troop. He took his corporalship very seriously, but was lively, full of fun, and a great favorite with the boys. In reading Kipling's "Soldiers Three," the character of Ortheris has always brought Corporal Rudd vividly to my recollection.

McKay was a splendidly built young athlete and as handsome as a Greek god. His running broad jump was the pride of the troop. He had a sweet tenor voice and sang old Scotch songs in a way to make homesickness epidemic at night about the campfires.

Corporal Williams, a royal good fellow, was known always as "Polly" Williams among the men. Horace Rowe was a small, dark, delicately made man. He was a poet of no mean order and had published a book of verse. Adams was also a poet, but rather of the cow-boy variety.

Durham was the wit of the company, and as brave a fellow as ever straddled a mustang. Rector was as deaf as a post, but was not lacking in nerve at any time. We used to yell at him in a way which he resented at times, and once I nearly had to fight a duel with him in consequence. Parrott was from the far-off banks of the Suwanee River, so famed in "The Old Folks at Home." I shall give an instance of his courage in another place. Watson was a lame fiddler, but a man of reckless bravery. Boyd had killed his man in Lower California and had escaped, by travelling on foot across Mexico, to Texas. Later, he went back to California, got out of his trouble there, and fell heir to a large estate. He was a handsome, jolly fellow and the best poker-player in the troop.

I remember how surprised I was, when we rode out from the camp near Laredo that first morning, to note the youth of Lieutenant Wright, who, mounted on a sturdy little black stallion, rode at the head of the troop. He certainly was very young to be second in command. I don't think he could have been more than nineteen years old at that time; but his face was a determined one, and he had a trick of drawing his eyebrows into a straight line and knitting his forehead above them which hardened his expression, and made him seem older than he actually was. His straight, thin mouth and firm chin denoted much character, and it did not take a very expert student of physiognomy to see that he was eminently fitted, despite his lack of years, to lead men into danger.

By his side, and chatting merrily with him, was a little boy, not more than ten years old. This boy was the Captain's son, and was known as "Rebel" among the boys, with whom he was a great favorite. It was only when we changed our base of operations that the Captain took his family on the march. Mrs. McNelly and her little daughter travelled in an ambulance, and the Captain was with them that morning, so let Reb ride his horse. Reb was as much at home in the saddle as any cow-boy. He was brimming over with mischief, and if he could get any of the men to lend him a six-shooter, took great delight in blazing away at trees, rabbits, or anything which chanced to cross his line of vision. As he was not a wonderful marksman, his target practice was, at times, a trifle dangerous to others.

Next to Lieutenant Wright was a long, lanky man, with a light sandy, sparse beard and long yellow hair. He was Sergeant Orrell, or, as the boys always called him, "Old Orrell," a Mississippian and as good-natured a fellow as ever breathed. Although continually talking about military discipline, he wisely confined his ideas to words, and never attempted to put them into practice. He was brave as a lion, and remarkably cool in a tight place, but was also very conceited, and as proud as a turkey-cock over his sergeantship. Rudd was almost as precise and martial in his notions as Orrell, but both of them knew the Rangers too well to try to enforce their notions upon the boys.

Armstrong was a Kentuckian and, like many of the sons of the Blue Grass State, was a giant in size. His sweeping blond mustache and pointed "goatee" would alone have made him conspicuous among so many beardless young men, but there was a good deal more to John B. Armstrong than his hirsute charms. He had a singularly mild blue eye, and experience on the frontier has taught me that mild blue eyes usually indicate anything but mildness of disposition. His handsome face was full of character. His carriage was as erect as that of a grenadier and, despite his great size, he was extremely graceful in all his movements. He was a dashing fellow, and always ready to lead a squad of the Rangers on any scout that promised to end in a fight.

The rest were, for the most part, beardless boys, full of deviltry and high spirits, and ready at a moment's notice to rush into any adventure, no matter how dangerous to life it might be. Their broad brimmed, picturesque, cow-boy hats, flannel shirts open at the throat, high boots, well-filled cartridge belts with dangling pistol holsters and bowie-knife scabbards, their carbines slung at the side of the saddles, their easy and perfect manner of riding, their sun-tanned faces, their general air of wild, happy, devil-may-care freedom and supreme confidence in themselves, showed that the Captain indeed chose wisely when he picked out the men for his dangerous mission.

Here were fellows who would not stop to count the cost beforehand, but would follow their leader with reckless enthusiasm, no matter where he might go. Such was the impression I received in looking at the Rangers that morning, nearly a quarter of a century ago, and it was correct. Only once since then have I seen any body of men which could be compared to the Rangers. I refer to Colonel Theodore Roosevelt's regiment of "Rough Riders," which did such magnificent work in Cuba under his command. And among the "Rough Riders" I met a number of ex-Texas Rangers, who had all given good accounts of themselves in the fighting before Santiago de Cuba.

Colonel Roosevelt has written in his story of "The Rough Riders" the following:

"We drew a great many recruits from Texas: and from nowhere did we get a higher average, for many of them had served in that famous body of frontier fighters, the Texas Rangers. Of course, these Rangers needed no teaching. They were already trained to obey and to take responsibility. They were splendid shots, horsemen and trailers. They were accustomed to living in the open, to enduring great fatigue and hardship, and to encountering all kinds of danger."

CHAPTER IX

ROVING VIGILANCE COMMITTEE DISBANDED
BY MC NELLY

And now for a more detailed story of the work of the command which I had joined as the result of such a queer series of adventures. I shall undertake to tell only of the more important scouts which were undertaken, with here and there a digression called up by the remembrance of some characteristic scene or noteworthy incident. I shall describe the Texas desperado of over a score of years ago, as I knew him. He may not be all that border fiction has painted him, but the description will have the merit of strict truth. Even at his tamest, he was sufficiently picturesque.

We went by easy stages across the country to Corpus Christi, the pretty little old town on the Gulf of Mexico. We were ordered there because Mexican raiders had come across the Rio Grande and spread terror throughout that part of Texas.

We arrived at Corpus Christi on the morning of April 22, 1875, and found the country in the wildest state of excitement. We were told how large bands of raiders were coming from every direction to lay waste the country-side and burn the town. The most extravagant rumors found ready credence from the terrorized people. The civil authorities seemed helpless. Large parties of mounted and well-armed men, residents of Nueces County, were riding over the country, committing the most brutal outrages, murdering peacable Mexican farmers and stockmen who had lived all their lives in Texas. These murderers called themselves vigilance committees and pretended that they were acting in the cause of law and order.

We remained encamped near the town for two days, to rest our jaded horses and to try to get a clear idea of the actual condition of affairs.

It seemed that the excitement had been first caused by a raid made by Mexicans (from Mexico) in the neighborhood of Corpus Christi. These raiders had stolen cattle and horses, burned ranch houses, murdered men and ravished women, and then escaped back to Mexico. The excitement which followed was seized upon by a number of white men living in Nueces County as a fitting time to settle up old scores with the Mexican residents of that and some of the adjoining counties. Many of these Mexicans, it must be admitted, had been making a livelihood by stealing and skinning cattle, and the sheriffs and constables had failed to make any efforts to detect and punish them.

On the evening of April 24th a report was brought in that a party of raiders from Mexico had been seen at La Para, about sixty miles from Corpus Christi. McNelly at once started with the troop to that place and arrived the following day. There we learned that the party reported to be Mexican raiders was really a posse of citizens from Cameron County, under a deputy sheriff, and that they "had come out to protect the people of La Para from further outrages from the citizens of Nueces County," meaning certain lawless bands organized in Nueces County.

McNelly ordered the deputy sheriff to take his posse back and disband it. After some demurring on the part of the posse, this was done. We went into camp and McNelly sent scouting parties out in every direction to disband the various vigilance committees and "regulators" which were roaming through the country.

On April 26th two companies of white men, commanded by T. Hynes Clark and M. S. Culver, cattlemen, came to our camp and said they wanted to co-operate with the Rangers.

"We need no one to co-operate with us," said the Captain. "I have heard that some of you men are the very ones accused of a number of outrages committed on Mexican citizens of this State, and you must disband at once and not re-assemble, except at the call and under the command of an officer of the State. If you don't do as I say, you will have us to fight."

The Texans didn't like this high-handed way of talking and were disposed at first to dispute McNelly's authority, but the Captain showed them very quickly that he meant business and they disbanded.

We remained in camp, constantly scouting in various directions, until matters had quieted down. When everything was quiet, we went to Edinburg, in Hidalgo County, and reached there on May 16th. On May 20th we moved down the Rio Grande.

We found the frontier in a state of great excitement. Reports of a dozen different raiding parties would be brought in daily and the scouting parties had no rest. I was in the saddle almost continually. At night we would either camp where we happened to be, or continue riding, in the attempt to head off some party of raiders of whom we had heard. Many of the reports of raiders brought to us were groundless, but the greater number were true. Through fear of the robbers, the law-abiding citizens withheld information which would have insured the capture of the marauders.

The people said that large droves of cattle and horses were stolen and driven across the Rio Grande into Mexico almost nightly. This, we found, had been going on for years. The United States military authorities had never made a determined effort to put a stop to the wholesale stealing, although the raiders at times would pass close to the frontier posts.

McNelly continued to keep out scouting parties of Rangers, and this course had the effect of lessing the number of raids, but not of wholly putting an end to them.

While we were camped at a place called Las Rucias, which we reached on June 5th, a Mexican brought the information to Captain McNelly that a party of raiders was crossing into Texas, below Brownsville, and going in the direction of La Para. Our camp was about twenty-five miles from Brownsville. Many Rangers were out on scouts at the time we received the information and but seventeen of the boys were in camp. This was on June 11th. McNelly at once ordered us to saddle up, and within fifteen minutes we were trotting after him and a Mexican guide over the prairie. Lieutenant Wright was in the party. So was Lieutenant Robinson.

We camped that night by a little, half-dried-up creek, and early the next morning a Mexican scout came in and said he had discovered the trail of the raiders. We ate a hurried breakfast and started out after the Mexican. In a short time we captured an advance scout of the raiders—one Rafael Salinas—and, by threatening him with instant death if he did not divulge what he knew of the robbers, we obtained much valuable information from him.

A little later we managed to catch another of the raiders and his story agreed with the one the first man had told us. This second scout said that the raiders had turned the cattle loose, as the men had become frightened when the first scout failed to return.

It was three days after that before we managed to head off the raiders. They had fourteen men and we had eighteen, including

Captain McNelly. We found them with the cattle on a little bit of wooded rising ground surrounded by a swamp called Laguna Madre. The water was eighteen or twenty inches deep in it.

They were drawn up in line and were evidently expecting us. When they saw us, they drew off behind the rising ground and fired at a range of about one hundred and fifty yards with carbines.

"Boys," said Captain McNelly, "the only way we can get at those thieves is to cross through the mud of the swamp and ride them down. I don't think they can shoot well enough to hit any of us, but we'll have to risk that. Don't fire at them until you're sure of killing every time."

Following the Captain, we started across the swamp for the little hill, the Mexican marauders continually firing at us. When we got near the hill, the Captain put spurs to his horse and we followed him with a yell as we flew through the mud and up the hill. The Mexicans answered our yell with one of defiance and a volley. At first, we thought they had not done any execution, but we soon saw they had aimed only too well, for three of our horses went crashing to the ground, one after the other, throwing their riders over their heads. Lieutenant Robinson's horse was one of those shot, but Robinson continued to fight on foot.

Then came a single shot from the Mexicans, and one of the Rangers—L. S. Smith, popularly known to the troop as "Sonny" —threw his arms above his head, reeled in his saddle for a moment and fell headlong to the ground. We all saw him fall and the sight roused a fury in our hearts that boded ill for the men in front of us.

The Mexicans fired at us again, but this time did no harm. The next instant we were upon them, shooting and yelling like demons. They stood their ground for a moment only; then turned and fled. As they went they leaned forward on their horses' necks and fired back at us, but they were demoralized by the fury of our onslaught and could hit nothing.

Crack! bang! bang! went our revolvers, and at nearly every shot one of the raiders went tumbling from his saddle. We had ridden hard to get to that place and our horses were played out, but we never thought of giving up the chase on that account. The remembrance of poor young Smith's face, as he threw up his hands and reeled from his horse, was too fresh in our minds for us to think of anything but revenge.

Some of our enemies were well mounted, but even these we gradually overhauled. We flew over the prairie at a killing pace, intent only on avenging our comrade's death. When we finally did halt, our horses were ready to drop from exhaustion; but the work had been done—every man of the raiders but one was dead. Some of them fought so desperately that even when dismounted and wounded four or five times they continued to shoot at us. Lieutenant Wright, during the running fight, killed two men with one shot from his revolver. The men were riding on one horse when he killed them and both were shooting back at him.

The leader of the raiders, Espiñoso, was thrown from his horse early in the fight. McNelly was after him and as soon as he saw Espiñoso fall he, too, sprang to the ground. Espiñoso jumped into a "hog wallow" in the prairie and McNelly took shelter in another one. Then they fought a duel. At last McNelly played a trick on the Mexican. The Captain had a carbine and a six-shooter. He aimed his carbine carefully at the top of Espiñoso's hog wallow and then fired his pistol in the air. Espiñoso raised his head, and the next instant a bullet from McNelly's carbine had passed through it and the Mexican bandit was dead.

Espiñoso was the most famous of the raiders on the Rio Grande and one of the head men under the Mexican guerilla chief, Cortina. Cortina was a Mexican General, and at the head of all the cattle raiding. He had a contract to deliver in Cuba six hundred head of Texas cattle every week. About three thousand robbers were under him, and he was virtually the ruler of the Mexican border.

When we rode back to the hill where we first met the raiders, we discovered that we had killed only thirteen of them. The fourteenth was terribly wounded. His name was Mario Olguine, nicknamed "Aboja." He was known to the Mexicans as Aboja (the Needle) because he had such a quiet way of slipping into ranch houses, on raids, and murdering the inmates while they slept. Aboja was sent to jail, but died there, after lingering several weeks. We recovered 265 stolen cattle after the fight. We procured a wagon and took the body of young Smith to Brownsville. The next day the bodies of the thirteen dead Mexicans were brought to Brownsville and laid out in the plaza. Nearly the entire population of Matamoras, the Mexican town immediately across the Rio Grande from Brownsville, came over to see their dead countrymen. The Mexicans were very angry, and we heard many threats that Cortina would come across with his men and kill us all. McNelly sent back word to Cortina that he would wait for him and his men. Cortina's bandits outnumbered the Rangers and the United States forces at Fort Brown about ten to one at that time.

We gave Smith a fine military funeral. The Mexican raiders were all buried in one trench. The Mexican inhabitants of the town stood in their doorways and scowled at us whenever we passed, but they were afraid to express their hatred openly. They contented themselves with predicting that Cortina would come over and kill us. Had they but known it, one of our men, Sergeant George Hall, a cousin of McNelly's, was at that very time with Cortina, acting as a spy for us. Hall was on Cortina's boat, waiting with him for the cattle to ship to Havana. In the records of the United States Government at Washington there is doubtless a most interesting report which Hall made to the Federal authorities, for General Grant, who was President at that time, sent for Hall and personally received his report.

Grant was greatly interested in Cortina's movements, and it was said among those who knew how matters stood on the border and in Washington, that the President would have been glad to have a war break out between Mexico and the United States. Of that I will speak more fully in another place.

Chapter X

GETTING A REPUTATION AS DAREDEVILS

At the time of which I write, Matamoras was full of Mexican soldiers, and Cortina had put the place under martial rule. No person was allowed on the streets after sunset, except by special permit; that is, no Mexican was allowed on the streets. For some reason best known to Cortina, Americans were not included in the rule, and the Mexican sentries had orders to pass Americans. The Rangers were not slow to take advantage of this state of affairs, and we paid frequent visits to Matamoras after nightfall. We went there for two reasons: to have fun, and to carry out a set policy of terrorizing the Mexicans at every opportunity. Captain McNelly assumed that the more we were feared, the easier would be our work of subduing the Mexican raiders; so it was tacitly understood that we were to gain a reputation as fire-eating, quarrelsome dare-devils as quickly as possible, and to let no opportunity go unimproved to assert ourselves and override the "Greasers." Perhaps everyone has more or less of the bully inhert in his make-up, for certain it is that we enjoyed this work hugely.

"Each Ranger was a little standing army in himself," was the way Lieutenant Wright put it to me, speaking, long afterward, of those experiences. The Mexicans were afraid of us, collectively and individually, and added to the fear was a bitter hatred.

Half a dozen of the boys would leave camp after dark and make their way over the river to Matamoras by way of the ferry. If we could find a *fandango*, or Mexican dance, going on, we would enter the dancing-hall and break up the festivities by shooting out the lights. This would naturally result in much confusion and, added to the reports of our revolvers, would be the shrill screaming of women and the cursing of angry Mexicans. Soldiers would come running from all directions. We would then fire a few more shots in the air and make off for the ferry, as fast as we could go.

Usually, at such times, we would be followed — at a safe

distance—by a company or two of soldiers. Sometimes we would fire back, over their heads, and sometimes they would shoot at us; but we always got back safely to the Texas side. When we reached Brownsville, we would hunt up another *fandango*—there were always some of these dances going on every night—and proceed, as in Matamoras, to break it up.

The news of our big fight with the raiders reached everyone's ears, and none was so bold as to attempt to resist our outrages upon the peace and dignity of the community, for such they undoubtedly were. But we accomplished our purpose. In a few weeks we were feared as men were never before feared on that border, and, had we given the opportunity, we should undoubtedly have been exterminated by the Mexicans, but there was "method in our madness," and we never gave them the chance to get the better of us.

A story was told in Brownsville, in relation to the orders to the Mexican soldiers in Matamoras to pass all Americans. It was said that, one night, an American cow-boy was reeling toward the ferry in Matamoras, where he had been looking too long upon the treacherous *mescal,* a most intoxicating beverage. The cow-boy had not gone far before a Mexican sentinel appeared out of the gloom and shouted:

"*Parete!*" (Halt!)

"Go to ———, you ——— black Greaser!"

"*Está bueno,*" said the sentinel, recognizing the answer as coming from an American, but not understanding the words; "*Pase Usted, Señor.*"

And he brought his musket to a "carry" as the cow-boy passed on, cursing him at every unsteady step.

One of our men came very near paying the penalty of his rashness, one night, at a *fandango* in Brownsville. He was passing a house when he heard the music of guitars and a violin and the voice of a Mexican shouting the figures of a dance. The Ranger knew that a *fandango* was in progress, and he made up his mind to put a stop to it. It was wonderful how opposed to dancing the Rangers had become. No religious fanatic was ever more active in discouraging round dances than were McNelly's men. The sound of a fiddle playing a waltz was, in its effect, like touching a match to a train of powder. It always roused the Rangers to prompt action, and in ten minutes, at the utmost, the twinkling feet of the dancers were hurrying away in every direction, as fast as wholesome fear could make them travel.

But, previous to the incident of which I write, we had always gone to work to break up the dances in parties from four to half a dozen men. No one had ever attempted to carry on the good work all by himself. But this particular Ranger—he was Boyd—did not wish to waste valuable time by going to camp and securing the assistance of some of the other discouragers of terpsichorean revels. Boyd made up his mind to go in and stop that *fandango* at once, and single-handed.

He accordingly turned aside and entered the adobe house where it was in progress. There were about fifty Mexicans in the place when Boyd entered, but a little thing like that was not sufficient to discourage him when he set his heart on doing a good, moral piece of work. Perhaps he had been glancing once or twice too often upon the *mescal* when it was yellow, but, be that as it may, he did something which no man in his senses would have attempted. He walked into the middle of the room where those fifty-odd "Greasers" were dancing and, pulling his revolver, deliberately proceeded to shoot at the lamps which were placed in brackets on the walls.

He had fired but three shots when something hit him on the head from behind and he dropped to the floor like a log. A dozen of the Mexicans were on him in an instant, hitting and kicking him, and he certainly would have been killed, then and there, if something hadn't happened opportunely to save him. That something was the entrance of six of the Rangers who were attracted by the noise of the shooting as they were passing the place. They ran in and made their way to the place where Boyd was being beaten. As soon as they recognized Boyd, they turned on his assailants.

The blood of the Mexicans was up, however, and they stood their ground. A fight ensued, and it was a bloody one. The Mexicans were all armed with knives, and some had pistols. The room was so crowded and there were so many women, that the Rangers would not shoot, but used their six-shooters as clubs. They succeeded in rescuing Boyd and running the Mexicans out of the place, but not until some heads had been broken. Fortunately, no one was killed.

This was such a serious affair that it made much talk in the town, and the result was Captain McNelly issued orders that no more *fandango* raids should be made.

It must not be supposed, however, that the Rangers had nothing to do, all this time, except terrorize the Mexicans. Some of the men were continually off on scouts of more or less importance. Occasionally, the boys would have a fight, but more often they would make arrests peaceably enough. Sometimes so many of the men were off on these scouts that not more than two or three would be left in camp at a time. I was almost constantly in the saddle. We did most of our riding at night. This was for two reasons; our movements at night did not attract so much attention, and then, in that hot climate, night-riding is less severe on horses than traveling under the blazing semi-tropical sun. It was on one of these night scouts that we obtained an important addition to the troop. He was a Mexican—the only one who ever belonged to the Ranger troop.

His name was Jesus Sandabol. In appearance he did not differ from hundreds of other Mexicans on that border, except that he was rather taller than the majority of them, and was also remarkably thin and angular. His eyes were as black as jet and singularly piercing. He was very sinewy and strong and as active as any man I ever saw. He could mount a pony without putting his hand on him at all. He would simply run alongside of the horse for a little way and spring into the saddle with a bound. I have seen this feat performed at a circus by expert bareback riders, but never with the ease with which Sandobal did it. Once mounted, he was an extremely graceful rider and a daring one.

He came to us as a guide, and after we learned his history we did not wonder that the Captain had made him a member of the troop, Mexican though he was. There was no fear that Sandobal would ever betray any of the Rangers to his countrymen. He had no country, in fact. He had renounced all allegiance to Mexico, and he hated the Mexicans with such a bitter, consuming hatred that his life was devoted to doing them all the injury possible.

One year before he became our guide, Jesus Sandobal was living at peace on his ranch in Texas, a few miles above Brownsville and near the Rio Grande. By hard work and attention to business, he accumulated quite a little fortune in horses and cattle, fenced in a few acres of ground, built himself a commodious adobe house, and was prosperous and happy. He was devoted to his wife and daughter, the latter a pretty girl of fifteen years.

He had had the advantage of a good education at a school in the City of Mexico, and was vastly superior in his tastes to any of the Mexicans with whom he was brought in contact on the border. He held himself somewhat aloof from them and, in consequence, was disliked by many. They resented his haughty bearing, and his air of condescension was galling to them. There was too much of the manner of the old-time Spanish *caballero* about him to suit their ideas. He probably knew this, but if so, the knowledge had no effect upon his way of treating his neighbors and others whom he met from day to day. He was always courteous to them, but he did not attempt to disguise the fact that he considered himself better than they.

One morning, Sandobal left his ranch to go on some business up the Rio Grande, near Ringgold Barracks, almost a hundred miles away. He kissed his wife and daughter affectionately and told them he would ride hard and be back with them in four days at the latest. He left his ranch in the care of a man named Juan Valdez, his chief *vaquero*. Valdez had been with Don Jesus for several months and had done his work well, although he seemed of a rather morose disposition. Sandobal trusted him fully.

On the evening of the fourth day from his departure from his ranch, Sandobal returned to it. When he reached a point within a mile of his house, he put spurs to his horse and galloped merrily on in his haste to see his loved ones again. In a few minutes he came within sight of his house, but when he turned his eyes toward it his heart sank within him. Instead of the neat dwelling which he had left a few days before, he saw a heap of ruins. He flew to the place. It was silent and deserted. His home had been destroyed by fire and its inhabitants were gone.

At first, he thought it had been accidentally burned and that his wife and daughter had merely gone to await his return at some neighbor's house, or in Brownsville, where they had relatives. But he did not think so long. Upon looking around, he found that his barn was burned, too. His fences were torn down. All his cattle had been driven off.

Then he knew what had happened. He had lived too long on that accursed border not to recognize the work of the dreaded Mexican raiders from across the Rio Grande. He knew that his ranch had been destroyed by them and that he was a ruined man.

But what had become of his wife and daughter? When he thought of them his heart grew sick, for well we knew the treatment which women had to expect from the raiders of the border. He turned his horse's head away from the ruins of his home and set out on a run for the nearest ranch-house. Its owner heard him coming and hurried to the gate.

"My wife—my little daughter, Antonita—where are they?" shouted Sandobal, as he pulled his horse up so suddenly that the animal reared back on its haunches.

The *ranchero* looked at Don Jesus and noted the terrible expression on his face—the drawn features and the fierce, glittering eyes—and for a moment he dared not answer him.

"For the love of the good God, speak!" said Sandobal in a hoarse, strained voice. "Do not keep me in suspense. Are they safe? Did they escape? Are they here?"

Still the *ranchero* was silent.

Suddenly Sandobal threw himself from his horse and strode straight up to the man. He looked the *ranchero* in the eyes with a searching stare for a moment; then he grasped him with his strong hands by both shoulders and shook him as a dog would a rat. Between his set teeth he spoke, saying:

"By God, you shall answer me, or I'll strangle you as I would a *cajote*."

Then the *ranchero* found words to answer him.

"Calm yourself, Senor," he said. "You hurt me. There; that is better. You must bear it like a man, Don Jesus, for there is terrible news for you. Your wife and daughter are alive, but——"

The *ranchero* hung his head and his eyes sought the ground. He could not tell the husband and father of the foul wrong which had been put upon his loved ones. But he had said enough. Sandobal knew that his worst fears were confirmed. After a pause of many minutes, he said, in a strangely calm voice for the expression which accompanied it:

"Where are they, *amigo mio?*"

"They have gone to the convent in Matamoras. They are with the holy Sisters."

Sandobal pressed his friend's hand with a strong grasp and turned from him without another word. The next minute he was on his horse galloping away toward his ruined ranch. Inquiries were made for him on the following day, but he had disappeared. It was learned that he had gone to the convent in Matamoras and there seen his wife and daughter. After he left the convent, all trace of him was lost.

In a few weeks, strange and terrible rumors spread throughout the lower Rio Grande border. It was said that, night after night, a different ranch was burned in Mexico, not far from the big river; that, day after day, some man was found dead on the road in the same neighborhood with a bullet-hole in his head; that the cattle in Mexico were dying of some new and strange disease; that horses were being killed by some unknown hand, and that persons drinking from wells and springs in Mexico had fallen violently ill and died in agony shortly after.

And, in all these cases, the persons who had been shot or poisoned were those who were known to belong to the bands of raiders who lived by their frequent depredations in Texas. It was their ranches which were burned; it was their cattle which died; it was their horses which were killed.

As time went on these awful happenings did not decrease in frequency. Indeed, they became of more frequent occurrence and the scene of them ever widened. The people became terror-stricken. Men banded together to hunt down their common, but unknown enemy. They scoured the country for him. They offered large rewards for his detection and capture, dead or alive. But it was all to no purpose. Every few nights a hitherto untouched ranch was set on fire; every day or two, another man was found dead with a bullet-hole in his temple. The cattle and the horses continued to die. Springs and wells, and even streams which emptied into the Rio Grande, were found to be poisoned.

For over eight months this kept up. Scores of ranches were burned; forty or fifty men were assassinated, and hundreds of horses and cattle died in that period. And in all that time Sandobal was absent from Texas, save for brief visits which he paid to Brownsville. When anyone would ask him where he was living and what he was doing, he would reply that he was "doing some work for the Mexican Government." He would make purchases of provisions and cartridges and leave the town again, not to return for another month or six weeks. On these occasional visits he always went to the convent in Matamoras, to see his wife and daughter.

Why the Mexicans did not sooner suspect Sandobal as the man who had been playing such havoc in Mexico near the border, I cannot imagine, but when, at last, they did couple his name with the outrages no one doubted that he was their perpetrator. The people had no direct proof that he was the man, but they felt sure of it as soon as it was suggested. A hunt began for him, but he could not be found. It was discovered, however, that he had not been employed by the Mexican Government in any capacity, and this tended to confirm the suspicions.

It was while the border country was ringing with Sandobal's name and the hunt for him was being prosecuted that he joined the Rangers as a guide. Of course, he denied that he had been taking such awful revenge for the wrongs done him, but none of us believed his denials. I have good reason to be convinced that Captain McNelly knew positively Sandobal was the dreaded border scourge, and I suspect that it was for that very reason he enlisted him in the troop.

Sandobal—we all called him Jesus* in the Company—was safe from molestation so long as he was with the Rangers, although direful threats regarding him reached us constantly. Sandobal merely smiled grimly when he heard the threats. His life was too bitter for him to care for them. For hours at a time he would sit in the camp with his back against a tree, brooding over his troubles and lost to all that was passing around him. When, however, any one of the Rangers spoke to him, he always answered in the pleasantest manner. He absolutely worshipped the Rangers and was ever ready to go to any trouble to please them, collectively or individually.

When any of the boys returned from a scout, he was always the first to greet them and to ask if they had killed any Mexicans. If the answer was in the negative, he would plainly indicate his disappointment, but if it was in the affirmative, his eyes would brighten, his lips would curve into a smile, and he would pat the men on the back and call them *"muy bravos hombres"* and say that he wished he had been with them. If a Mexican prisoner was brought into camp, he was always as carefully guarded to keep Sandobal from doing him an injury as to prevent his escape. This was particularly the case after one of the prisoners complained that Sandobal had threatened to hang him at the first opportunity. I do not doubt that our guide would have done so had he had the chance.

But Sandobal's hunger for revenge on the Mexican raiders was

*Pronounced in Spanish, Hay-soos with the accent on the last syllable.

destined to be glutted before he left the Rangers, for he was to take part in the most exciting and dangerous scout which the Rangers ever undertook, the story of which rang throughout all Texas, and the effect of which was practically to break up the border-thieving on the lower Rio Grande for many months, or so long as McNelly's troop remained in that part of the country.

Chapter XI

THE COMMAND CROSSES THE RIO GRANDE

For months we continued to scout from Fort Brown to Rancho Davis and far up the Rio Grande, and the cattle-thieves grew more and more cautious, for they knew that the Rangers were in that country for business and would not hesitate to kill them on sight. Late in June we left our camp near Brownsville and went to Santa Maria, thirty-five miles farther up the river, where we heard a party of raiders had crossed to Texas. The robbers heard of our coming and fled to Mexico.

We were so constantly moving from one place to another, by night as well as day, that the raiders never knew where we would appear and, for the first time in many years, they were checked in their work. Another good effect of our ceaseless activity and vigilance was that the Mexican settlers on the Texas side of the Rio Grande no longer co-operated with the raiders by withholding information from us and giving it to them. These settlers seemed to realize that a new condition had arisen, and that the State of Texas was determined on a different course from that which had theretofore been pursued on the line of the border.

On August 4th we received reliable information that a band of forty of the robbers were to be at a certain place in Hidalgo County in three days. We prepared to go to meet them and give them a warm reception; but before we started, a scout came in and told us that the leader of the gang had been assasinated by 'one of his own men on the day they were to start for Mexico, and that the raid had been abandoned. Investigation showed this to be true.

About the middle of August we moved back from the Rio Grande, so as to entice the raiders over and give them a few more lessons on the danger of invading Texas, and we continued to hunt them with more or less success until November, when we had "the big fight."

We were encamped, November 20th, at Ratama ranch, about forty miles north of the Rio Grande. Lieutenant Robinson was in command, the Captain having gone to the Rio Grande to reconnoitre. There were about thirty of the boys in camp, lounging about, practicing with their six-shooters at trees and betting with each other on their marksmanship, playing poker with grains of corn for "chips" and a blanket spread on the ground for a table, or cleaning and polishing their carbines and revolvers, when a Mexican rode hurriedly up and asked to see Lieutenant Robinson.

"I'm Robinson; what do you want?" demanded the Lieutenant.

The Mexican handed him a note which Robinson hurriedly read. The men knew that something serious was up from the officer's face and gathered around him. Robinson looked up from the note.

"Saddle up, boys," he said. "Don't waste any time about it, for we must be off immediately. We can't wait for dinner. Take what grub you can find that's cooked and bring it along with you. Be sure and girth your horses tight, for you can't stop to do it on the road. We're in for some fun this time, sure. Take all the cartridges you can carry."

The Rangers gave a yell of delight and started on a run for their horses, which were herded close to the camp. In a marvelously short time we had made them ready, and when, in less than ten minutes, Robinson gave the order to "fall in," every man was in his saddle and alert.

"Now, Jesus," said Lieutenant Robinson to Sandobal, "take us by the nearest road you know to Los Cuevos; the raiders are there, fighting the United States troops."

Sandobal's face lighted up with a great joy, and he darted to the front of the column and away toward the south at a gallop. As we swung out after him, the sun was shining directly over our heads. It was exactly noon.

We took an old, unused trail which the recent rains had washed out in many places, and it was very muddy. It would have been a bad road to ride on a walk, but it was doubly so at the rate we went. From a gallop to a sharp trot, and back again to a gallop, we went, hour after hour, stopping every five or six miles for a very few minutes to breathe our horses. We did not go at a walk at all. The mud flew up and plastered the men from head to foot and the horses were coated with it, but we did not pause or slacken the pace.

Sandobal, closely followed by the Lieutenant, rode ahead, and we followed in a long, straggling line. Most of the way it was imposible for the men to ride two abreast and we went in single file. Mile after mile we rode, at this killing pace, under the hot Texas sun, and I thought that some of the ponies would drop from exhaustion, but none did. The men were all toughened to hard riding, and did not mind it in the least.

Los Cuevos, we learned from Sandobal, was sixty miles away, and it was evidently the intention to reach there that day. Such an undertaking, even on a good road, would have been tremendous, but on that old, rain-washed trail it seemed impossible of accomplishment.

But we did it. Just as the sun was sinking below the mesquite-covered prairie to the west we arrived at the place. Sixty miles on a bad trail between noon and sundown! Such riding as that had not before been done by a body of men on that border, and I have never heard of it being equalled elsewhere. Horses and men were alike exhausted, and when we stopped we threw ourselves from the saddles and stood by our panting, dripping ponies, glad to get the rest which the change of position gave us.

We had stopped on the bank of the Rio Grande close to the water. All about us the mud was ankle deep, and marked with the hoofprints of hundreds of cattle. At the other side of the river we could just make out in the gathering gloom—for the twilights are very short in that latitude—a flat-boat, tied to the bank. As we looked across the quarter of a mile of water which separated us from Mexico, we saw the boat swing out from the shore and go drifting down the river, and as it did so there came a yell of defiance and derision from the raiders over there. They had crossed all the stolen cattle and horses, and then had turned the flat-boat adrift to keep us from following on our horses.

As we stood watching them and wondering just what to do, we heard a sudden pounding of many hoofs, and the clanking of steel and creaking of leather, the unmistakable sounds of galloping horsemen. The sounds grew louder and closer. They were on our side of the river. The same thought must have flashed through the mind of every Ranger there, for, with a precision like that of men at drill, all turned to their saddles, yanked their carbines from the scabbards, and turned to fight the oncoming horsemen.

"Don't fire, boy; it's the Eighth Cavalry!" yelled Sergeant

Armstrong, who was in advance, and the Rangers dropped the carbines to their sides and carefully uncocked them.

Armstrong was right. In another minute thirty men of Troops H and M, Eighth United States Cavalry, under Captain James F. Randlett, with Lieutenant Farnsworth second in command, came dashing out of the brush and halted where we stood. They had left Brownsville at 1 A. M., November 18th, two days before. It took them all that time to come about the same distance we travelled in half a day! No better illustration of the difference between the methods of the Rangers and the regular cavalry could be given. We dared to kill our horses by hard riding, and they did not, which meant the difference between success and failure in the pursuit and capture of border-thieves.

Still, we all arrived too late that night to catch the raiders on this side of the Rio Grande, and Rangers and regulars condoled with each other heartily. It was more than provoking to us, who had taken such a terrible ride to head the thieves off, but there was no help for it. We scattered up and down the river-bank to look for a boat but after an hour's search, gave it up. There was no fodder or grazing for our poor horses, and they had to be content to eat the leaves from the mesquite brush to which we tied them.

About nine o'clock Captain McNelly rode up and joined us. He said he had left Major Alexander with two more troops of the Eighth Cavalry farther down the river, and that they would arrive, he thought, about dawn, together with Lieutenant Merritt and a detachment of the Twenty-fourth Infantry, with a Gatling gun.

Captain McNelly told us that the thieves we were after were under contract to deliver 18,000 head of cattle in Monterrey, Mexico, within ninety days, and that they had started to gather them in Texas. He said that Corinto had organized all the cattle-thieves in Mexico for this purpose, and that he really intended an invasion of Texas. It was clearly our duty to follow the robbers into Mexico, give them battle, and so nip their plans in the bud. He had received assurances that Major Alexander would instruct his men to follow the Rangers wherever they went.

That McNelly had good reason to believe Major Alexander would support him fully, even to the extent of crossing the border and following the marauders into Mexico, there can be no doubt. I knew that our Captain had been in direct communication with

President Grant regarding the Mexican outrages, and I, in common with many others, obtained the impression that Grant would welcome the chance to invade the Republic directly to the south of us. I know also that Major D. R. Clendennin, of the Eighth Cavalry, who was with the troops at Los Cuevos, as well as Major Alexander and Colonel Potter, commanding the District of the Rio Grande, understood that McNelly was to lead both the Rangers and the United States troops into Mexico. I speak of this matter here, so that the reader may understand under what conditions our Captain acted, and so that his bitter disappointment at the failure of Secretary of War Belknap to back up his actions may be appreciated.

That night we managed to catch two goats, which we killed and ate for supper. They were very tough, but we were very hungry, and we enjoyed them, although we had no bread or coffee.

At about eleven o'clock McNelly told Captain Randlett he thought it would be well to cross the Rio Grande, so as to be in position to move on the raiders early in the morning. Captain Randlett replied that he would have to await the arrival of Major Alexander before he took the United States troops across the border.

Then it was that Parrott, of our troop, did a most courageous thing. He undressed on the river-bank and swam the Rio Grande to try to find a boat on the other side in which we could cross. We waited quietly for word from him for fully half an hour, and at the end of that time were startled to hear him bawl across the river at the top of his lungs that he had secured a row-boat and would come right over. The wonderful "nerve" displayed by Parrott in yelling to us while he was on the other side of the river and surrounded by the Mexican desperadoes, impressed even the foolhardy Rangers, and he was ever after a hero in the troop.

He came back all right with the boat, and then Captain McNelly got into it with two of the men and started across the stream. Parrott's call had roused the Mexicans and they had probably discovered the loss of the boat, for we could hear them shouting and cursing on the opposite bank. So, when McNelly started across, we and the Eighth Cavalry troopers formed in line along the bank and prepared to shoot if McNelly was attacked when he reached the other side. We knelt in the mud, with our carbines ready to fire if it should be necessary.

Suddenly, from the opposite bank, whither McNelly and his

two men had gone, came the sound of a rifle-shot and the flash
of the gun. Instantly we blazed out with a volley from our carbines, firing at the flash. Before we could shoot again, we heard
the Captain shouting at us.

"For God's sake, don't fire!" he yelled. "Do-o-on't fire!"

We couldn't understand what he meant by such an order at the
time, but afterward we found out that one of the men who were
with him in the boat let his carbine go off accidentally as he
stepped to the shore. Luckily, we overshot them, but they said our
bullets sang very close to their ears.

McNelly and his two men reconnoitred along the bank, but
failed to find any of the Mexicans, and then one of the men
rowed back and we crossed the river, three at a time. Armstrong
swam his own horse over, and he was followed by four of the
others, but the water was very cold and the quicksands near the
bank made this a dangerous proceeding, so the rest of the Rangers
left their horses on the Texas side.

We lay on the ground over there, near the river-bank, that
night, with no covering whatever, although the night was raw
and chilly. We were tired, cold, dirty and wet; but, excepting the
men on guard, all slept soundly until a little before daylight. Then
McNelly had us quietly awakened. He sent across the river to
see if Major Alexander had arrived and to find out if he would
cross with his cavalry to Mexico. The messenger returned with
the information that Alexander had not yet arrived.

Then the Captain formed us in double ranks and, in a low
voice, made us a speech.

"Boys," he said, "I was expecting the United States soldiers
to help us in this fight, but I guess we'll have to go it alone now,
if we want to do anything before the robbers get away into the
interior. I want to tell you, right now, that I'll probably have to
lead you into hell for awhile, but I believe I can lead you out
again, all right. Still, if there is any man here who doesn't want
to come with me, he is at perfect liberty to say so and go back.
I won't treasure it up against him, for none of you boys enlisted
to fight in Mexico, and you needn't do it if you don't want to."

The Captain paused, but not a man moved or said anything.

"That is just what I expected of you," he went on, in a tone
of satisfaction. "Now I'll tell you what we have to do. About
a mile from here is the notorious Rancho de Los Cuevos, the
headquarters of the Mexican raiders. In that ranch are fine stores

of all kinds—silver-mounted bridles and saddles, carved weapons, fine horses. We want to capture the ranch. It is the head-quarters of a gang of ruffians who have lived off the United States for years and years. They have brought up their children to hate us and to prey upon our country. They have murdered our ranchmen and ruined thousands of homes in Texas. Now is our chance to get even. Doubtless, there are many men at the ranch, armed and ready for us. They are expecting our attack, for I sent word to their leader, some time ago, that if he ever made another raid into Texas, we would come over and take his ranch. We will have to fight and they will probably make a desperate resistance, but we can whip them.

"I know the kind of men you are. I know that your courage is unquestioned and I know that there are no better shots in Texas than you. You have plenty of ammunition and, by keeping cool and listening to orders and obeying them strictly, you can take that ranch. We are going to attack it at the crack of day, and when we do I want you to shoot every man you see and to spare none but the women and children. I want to make an example of these thieves and murderers and ravishers, and I depend on you to help me do it."

It was a rather long speech, that of the Captain's, but it was all to the point, and at its conclusion we knew just what we had to expect. The Captain had a way of taking his men into his confidence at such times, and they appreciated it and served him all the better for it.

When he had finished speaking, we moved slowly after him, along a narrow path through the willows and brush. The path was only a cattle-trail, and it led directly away from the river. We marched in single file. Ahead of the Captain was a Mexican guide who was to show the way to the ranch. We marched in dead silence, treading carefully through the underbrush so as to make the slightest sound. Armstrong and three others rode their horses and followed directly after those on foot. Jesus Sandobal was also mounted.

Just at the peep of day we came to a fence across the road. The troop halted there, and the Captain walked back along the line and told Armstrong that there was a gate in the fence a little below where we were. He told Armstrong that he wanted him and the other mounted men to go through that gate and ride through the ranch carefully, and then come back and report how matters stood. If they ran across any men, they were to shoot them.

"Shoot at everything you see," was the Captain's order.

"Yes, sir," answered Armstrong.

McNelly walked back to the head of the line and Armstrong, followed by the other mounted men, rode by us in the path. As they passed, I heard George Hall, who was on a horse, say to Armstrong:

"Armstrong, the Captain's going to have us killed."

"I guess that's right," answered Armstrong, "but we're in for it now and we'll have to stand it."

"Sure," said Hall.

Notwithstanding the seriousness of the situation, the Rangers who were on foot could not resist the temptation to poke fun at the mounted men.

"Good-by, if I never see you again," one whispered.

"Say, Armstrong, bring me a scalp, please," said another.

"I want one of those fancy saddles, covered with gold, Hall; be sure to save one for me before you die," came in soft accents from a third.

"You boys are going to hell in a hand-basket this time—better think of your sins," was the encouraging advice from a fourth.

The Captain went with the mounted Rangers and let down the bars at the gate for them. Then he came back to us. Armstrong led the men with him right into the ranch, six-shooter in hand. From him and the others I learned afterwards how they fared.

They went about a hundred yards beyond the fence and came to where the road forked. There they found five Mexican soldiers on guard as pickets. The Mexicans called to the Rangers to halt, and were answered with pistol-shots. Armstrong rode right on to them and the others followed. There was some quick shooting on both sides, at the end of which the five Mexican soldiers lay dead.

The five Rangers went straight on and shortly met two other Mexicans, who fired at them. They killed the Mexicans and continued to ride ahead.

Of course, we heard all this firing, and the Captain was quick to act accordingly. He sent half of the troop, with Lieutenant Robinson, to the right flank, and with the rest followed after the mounted men. I was in the Captain's squad. By the time we reached the place where the five dead men lay, the fog was so thick that we couldn't see ten yards ahead. Lieutenant Robinson had circled in and his detachment joined us at that place. They would have fired at us, too, at first if Sergeant L. L. Wright hadn't recognized us in time and prevented it. We were still at this spot when Armstrong came dashing up on his horse.

"We've taken the place, Captain," he cried exultantly. "The ranch is ours! We killed all the men we saw—seven of them."

"Seven?" exclaimed Captain McNelly. "Seven? There must be more than seven of them. I think there is some mistake. Let's go on."

We went ahead until we came to a ranch-house a short distance from where we had stopped. A woman was standing in the doorway patting a *tortilla,* or Mexican pancake, in her hand.

"What ranch is this?" demanded the Captain.

"Las Cucharas," answered the woman.

"Where is el Rancho de Los Cuevos?"

"Poco mas abajo, Señor." (A little further below, sir.)

Then our spirits went down to zero. We tried to be cheerful, but the outlook was gloomy for taking the thieves' ranch by surprise, as we had intended. All the shooting must have put its defenders very much on the alert, we knew, and our task, at no time an easy one, was rendered ten times more difficult.

We met a little boy as we were moving slowly along the road the woman had told us led to the Los Cuevos ranch. The little boy was driving a *burro,* laden with goatskins of water.

We asked him where the Los Cuevos ranch was and he, too, said:

"Poco mas abajo," but he added that there were many men and soldiers there.

We moved along like a funeral procession, for we knew that we had, by our shooting, given fair warning of our approach. About half a mile's march brought us at last to the Los Cuevos ranch. There was no mistaking it when we got there. As soon as we came in sight of the houses we were met by a storm of bullets from the corrals, built of thick mesquite and ebony logs, and bullet-proof. We were also greeted with yells and Mexican oaths and abuse of the vilest character.

We halted in the brush, about two hundred yards from the corrals, and for a few minutes returned the enemy's fire; but the fog grew much thicker and soon hid them from sight. Their bullets continued to pass over our heads. The four mounted men sat on their horses to the right of our line and watched the performance with interest, but did not attempt to take part in it. They were waiting for orders.

At one time during the firing I remember to have seen Durham taking very deliberate aim at a shadowy form far ahead, as though he were shooting at a squirrel. There was something so wonderfully cool and collected in his way of shutting one eye and squinting along the barrel of his carbine that it impressed me as comical and I actually shook with laughter at him, although I know the general run of my thoughts was in a very serious channel.

While we were waiting and wondering what the Captain would next order us to do, a troop of the famed Mexican Rurales, or bandit cavalry, dashed out from the corrals and came directly for our line on the full charge.

We gave them a volley as they came, and they swung around to the left in a semi-circle.

"Pick off your men, boys," shouted Captain McNelly. "I'll kill that fellow riding ahead myself."

The Captain's Winchester cracked, and the leader of the Rurales pitched from his saddle. A number of his followers' saddles were emptied quickly and the rest of the cavalrymen galloped off out of sight. About twenty-five men were in their troop.

There were evidently so many more of the Mexicans than there were of us that the Captain was puzzled how to act. He called George Hall to him and told him to ride up on a little rising ground, near the corrals, and try to estimate the number of men at the ranch. Hall did as ordered, riding under fire all the time. He came back in a few minutes and reported that, as near as he could estimate, about two hundred Mexicans were in sight in the corrals.

"I couldn't see very well, though," he said, "and I may be mistaken as to the number."

The Captain immediately despatched Armstrong to go closer still and see if he could make an estimate. Armstrong galloped off and went a little closer than Hall had gone. Soon he came dashing back and reported that he estimated there were about three hundred men in the corrals, and that many of them were in the uniforms of the regular Mexican cavalry.

"Then you think they outnumber us about ten to one?" said McNelly.

"That, or more," answered Armstrong.

Captain McNelly pulled a long black cigar from his pocket and put it between his teeth. He chewed on the end of it for a minute, in a brown study. Then he turned to the men and said:

"Boys, we are in a dangerous position here and we'd better get back to the river. We only have thirty men and they may get reinforcements at any time. We'll fall back slowly and I shall expect you gentlemen on the horses to keep the Mexicans off our rear."

We started back, expecting at every step that the entire Mexican force would be down on us and that we should have to make a desperate fight for our lives. But, luckily for us, the Mexicans suspected a trick and thought we were trying to draw them on to lead them into an ambush. The main body, then, did not follow us immediately, but sent scouts after us, who continually exchanged shots with our little rear guard. By the time we reached the river, however, the Mexicans saw that we were actually in retreat and not playing a trick on them. Then they charged on us.

They came down on us, yelling like devils and shooting rapidly, but we had strung out along the river-bank then, behind a little rise in the prairie, which gave us a sort of rude rifle-pit, and we met them with a murderous fire.

"Pick off the leaders, men!" cried Captain McNelly. "Don't waste a shot! Kill their leaders!"

We did so. We saw man after man tumble from his saddle, and then we heard the rattle of carbines from the Texas side of the river and the music of Lieutenant Merritt's Gatling gun. The United States troops were firing over our heads at the enemy.

It was too much for the Mexicans, and they wheeled and dashed back into the brush in full retreat, leaving the Alcalde of Camargo, Juan Flores, and a number of others dead on the field. These bodies lay in full sight from our lines, on a little open space which was free from the chaparral. The Mexicans formed in line on the other side of this open ground, and all the morning we kept up the firing, back and forth, across it. Twice they dashed out and tried to recover the body of the dead Alcalde of Camargo, but both times we drove them back quickly.

Chapter XII

ABANDONED BY THE ARMY

During the morning a number of the officers of the Eighth Cavalry came over to us and joined in the firing, but they took the precaution to remove their coats, on which were their shoulder-straps, before coming, so as not to appear with us in an official capacity. They wanted the excitement of the fighting and they wanted to help us against the superior number of the Mexicans, but they were with us without orders, Major Alexander having refused to cross the Rio Grande with his soldiers without direct instructions from Washington.

Among the officers of the Eighth who came thus "unofficially" to our assistance was Captain S. B. M. Young, the same man who, as Brigadier-General of Volunteers, commanded the Second Brigade, U. S. A., in the recent Santiago de Cuba campaign. Roosevelt's Rough Riders were in Young's brigade, and it was by Young's orders that the fight at Las Guasimas, the first battle of the Santiago campaign, was made.

Henry Guy Carleton, the playwright and litterateur, who comes of a long line of fighters, was a lieutenant in the Eighth Cavalry, and was also with the command under Major Alexander. He it was who, by order of Major Alexander, tapped the telegraph wire which ran along the Texas bank of the Rio Grande and established direct communication in the afternoon with the office of the Secretary of War at Washington.

About three o'clock in the afternoon a messenger came across the river, bearing a telegraphic despatch for Captain McNelly. I am able to give it and the answer it received, verbatim. The despatch handed to Captain McNelly was in Lieutenant Carleton's writing and was as follows:

FORT BROWN, November 20, 1875.

To MAJOR ALEXANDER,
    Commanding at the Front.
Advise Captain McNelly to return at once to this side of the

river. Inform him that you are directed not to support him in any way while he remains on Mexican territory. If McNelly is attacked by Mexican forces on Mexican ground, do not render him any assistance. Keep your forces in the position you hold now and await further orders. Let me know if McNelly acts upon your advice and returns.

(Signed)   POTTER,
Commanding District of the Rio Grande.

By order of the Secretary of War.

McNelly was white with anger when he read this despatch. He had received secret instructions from the Commanding General of the Department of Texas to follow the thieves into Mexico and, at the same time, had assurances that he would be supported in such action by the United States troops. He knew that both Colonel Potter and Major Alexander had seen his instructions. He had depended on their support when he crossed the Rio Grande so bravely with thirty Texas Rangers. Now that he was on Mexican soil and attacked, he was deserted "by order of the Secretary of War" (Belknap). He was mad right through. He took a bit of torn brown wrappingpaper and a stub of a pencil, and wrote this in reply.

At the Front near Los Cuevos, Mexico,
November 20, 1875.

To Colonel Potter,
    Commanding District of the Rio Grande,
        Fort Brown, Texas.

I shall remain in Mexico with my Rangers until to-morrow morning—perhaps longer, and shall recross the Rio Grande at my own discretion. Give my compliments to the Secretary of War and tell him the United States troops may go to hell.

(Signed)   L. H. McNelly,
Commanding Texas State Troops, Mexico.

In the official reports of this affair, on file in the office of the Adjutant-General of Texas in Austin, is the following from Major D. R. Clendennin, Eighth Cavalry, to Adjutant-General Steele:

I did not deem it best to interfere with McNelly, who had secret instructions from the Commanding General, Department of Texas, which Colonel Potter, commanding the District, had seen, as had also Major Alexander, of my regiment.

(Signed)   D. R. Clandennin,
                                Major Eighth Cavalry.

When Captain McNelly last saw Major Alexander, before our raid, the latter said to him:

"If you are determined to cross, we will cover your return, if we do not cross to help you" (vide official reports), but in spite of this promise, Captain McNelly and the Rangers were told officially in the telegram given above that they would have to get out of their predicament as best they could.

Captain McNelly showed us the message he received and explained the situation to us. The men felt as bitter in their anger as did the Captain. Like the Captain, they expressed themselves vigorously by saying, "Let the United States soldiers go to hell; we'll stay and fight it out by ourselves."

We were not all alone, however, for the United States army officers who were with us "unofficially," remained with us, and a few of the troopers of their regiment also contrived to come over to our assistance. They said they "gloried in our spunk."

The firing slacked up about 3:30 o'clock and we could find nothing to shoot at. The Mexicans were out of sight in the brush and had ceased firing almost entirely. McNelly put up with this inactivity for about half an hour, and that was so long as he could stand it.

"Let's get out into the open and draw their fire," he said, coolly, to Armstrong. "Then we can see what to shoot at."

The next minute he and Armstrong were walking deliberately out in the open space between the lines, just as though there were no Mexican bandits or soldiers within a hundred miles of them. They strolled leisurely to and fro, far out from our lines, but not a shot was fired at them. After awhile they came back to us, and then McNelly went over to Texas to send despatches, leaving Lieutenant Robinson in charge of the troop.

I know that McNelly attempted to establish direct communication with President Grant when he crossed the Rio Grande, for our Captain knew better than any other man at the front how Grant felt about the Mexican border outrages. He was certain the President would back him up in his action in crossing, for that his "secret instructions" had been inspired by the Silent Man in the White House was an open secret to all concerned in the Los Cuevos affair.

Before McNelly could reach the President by wire, however, we were surprised to see a flag of truce carried out from the Mexican lines, and a man was at once sent by Lieutenant Robinson to the Captain to request his return. With the flag of truce were five men. They rode half-way to our lines and halted, and Lieutenant Robinson detailed Armstrong and four men to go out and see them and find out what they wanted.

The leader of the Mexicans with the flag of truce was an American. He was a tall, handsome man, about forty years old, but his hair and long beard were as white as snow, giving him a most patriarchal appearance at a little distance. A closer view showed he had a youthful, ruddy complexion and deep, soft blue eyes. He wore a fine white linen suit and a broad white *sombrero*. He introduced himself as Dr. Headly.

With a bow of much courtliness, he handed Armstrong a carbine with a letter fastened to it under its hammer. Then he said in English:

"We have come to treat with you, gentlemen, and that is our communication to your commanding officer."

"The commanding officer is on the other side of the river," said Armstrong. "We have sent for him and he will be here soon."

"Where shall we await him?"

"Right here, where we are."

"Very well," said Dr. Headly, "but, in the meantime, suppose we take a smile."

He put his hand in the nosebag tied to his saddle and drew forth a bottle of *mescal,* which he politely offered to Armstrong.

"Thank you," said Armstrong, "but I cannot drink while I am on duty."

The white-bearded doctor raised his eyebrows in the mild surprise and offered the bottle to each of the other Rangers, but all declined to drink.

"Ah," said Dr. Headly; then with a bland smile, "you gentlemen must be afraid of poison. I am an American myself, and I would not play such a trick as that upon you, and to convince you that the liquor is all right, I here drink to your good health."

He suited his action to his words and drank from the bottle. Then his Mexican companions, two of whom were in officers' uniforms, drank from the bottle, each in Spanish politely wishing the good health of the Rangers. When they had all drunk, the doctor again handed the bottle to Armstrong, but again it was politely declined. The handsome doctor then became very talkative and asked Armstrong a number of questions, but Armstrong told him he was under orders not to converse with him and begged to be excused.

Presently Captain McNelly came, and the letter fastened to the carbine was handed to him. While he was reading it, the Mexicans and their American leader drew off a little distance. The Captain was still reading the communication when one of our men came hurrying from our lines with a message to Armstrong from Lieutenant Robinson. The messenger whispered something to Armstrong and waited.

"What's up?" called out Captain McNelly, who had observed the action.

"Lieutenant Robinson sends word that the enemy are advancing," cried Armstrong in a voice loud enough for all to hear. "He says the Mexicans are advancing on our right. He can hear them close by, in large numbers, and he expects the firing to begin at any minute."

"Very well," said the Captain; "instruct your men to kill every one of this flag-of-truce party if there is a shot fired."

Dr. Headly, who heard all that passed, seemed greatly perturbed.

"My God!" he cried; "Captain, you don't intend to have us murdered, do you?"

"My men will obey my orders; you may call it what you please," answered McNelly.

"But," said Dr. Headly, "our troops have orders not to fire and not to advance while the flag of truce is here. Some of them have been drinking hard, and it may be that some reckless, drunken fellow will shoot; but, I can assure you, there will be no attack. I must insist upon you countermanding that order to your men. It isn't fair, while we are standing under a flag of true, to shoot us down like dogs."

McNelly looked Headly full in the eyes and answered:

"The life of one of my men is worth more than one thousand such as yours and your fellows. We are not here for fun."

"Well, will you permit me to send one of our officers back to prevent any accident of this kind?" asked Dr. Headly.

"Yes," said McNelly; "and I should advise him to hurry."

Headly spoke some words to one of the officers with him, and the Mexican hastened away. He seemed very glad to have the chance to get off, for he and his companions fully understood the Captain's orders, Dr. Headly having translated them for their benefit. After the officer had disappeared in the brush, Dr. Headly turned to McNelly, and said:

"Do you know how many of our men you have killed?"

"No," said the Captain.

"You have killed twenty-seven already," asserted Dr. Headly, gravely; "and this matter is getting serious. It is time some settlement was made. You have invaded our country and attacked the citizens and soldiers of your sister Republic, and————"

"Stop!" commanded McNelly, abruptly. "I am not here to listen to any long-winded harangue. We have come here to recover horses and cattle which your men have stolen from Texas. If you return them, we shall go back to Texas; otherwise, we shall stay here in Mexico."

"How many men have you?" asked Dr. Headly. "I may as well tell you that three regiments of Mexican troops are on their way here from Monterey and from Matamoras to drive you out of Mexico."

"Yes? Well, you'll need them all," said McNelly, with a smile.

"Why, how many men have you?"

"Enough," said the Captin, "to march from here to the City of Mexico, if necessary."

It was a beautiful bluff, and it worked. The treating party lost no more time in coming to terms. It was quickly arranged that all the stolen stock should be turned over at ten o'clock the following morning to the Rangers at Rio Grande City—fifteen miles farther up the river. When Dr. Headly and the others had signed a paper to that effect, the Mexicans were permitted to carry away their dead.

Just at sunset we all recrossed the Rio Grande, and very glad we were to be once more on Texas soil.

We were tired and hungry, but we were happy, for we had won a big victory. With thirty men we had gone five miles on foot into Mexico, fought over ten times our number, killed twenty-seven of the enemy, brought them to terms and reached Texas again without the loss of a man. The Mexicans said afterward that they would certainly have annihilated us in Mexico had they known how few we were; but they never thought for an instant that we would be such fools as to invade their country with but thirty men to fight three or four hundred.

That night we had some of a freshly killed cow for supper. Epicures will tell you that beef is not fit to eat until it has been kept a number of days after being killed, but I never remember to have tasted any better than we had that night. We cooked it by thrusting a sharpened stick through a piece of it and broiling it in front of a camp-fire. We had no salt, but our appetites furnished the seasoning, and the supper was delicious to us.

After supper Captain McNelly told Armstrong to pick out fifteen of the horses best able to travel and take their riders up the river, so as to be at Rio Grande City in the morning in time to receive the cattle. The poor horses were all nearly famished, but we managed to get fifteen that would go the fifteen miles required, and started off that night, arriving at Rio Grande City before daylight. McNelly went with us. We camped outside the town and gave our horses some much-needed grazing.

In the morning we got breakfast at Rio Grande City, and, at ten o'clock, started down to the ford to receive the cattle. All the townspeople and the soldiers stationed at the nearby post knew what we had come for, and the bluffs on the river-bank were lined with people.

At the ford we met a small boy who told us he had a note for us from the commanding officer of the Mexican soldiers at Camargo. McNelly read the note. It was long and, with much circumlocution, stated that as it was Sunday, it was not customary or proper to transact business, and so the cattle would not be turned over to us until the following day, Monday.

McNelly wrote an answer to the note, in which he said he had arranged to receive the cattle that Sunday morning; that he had negotiated with officers—soldiers, and had supposed that they were gentlemen. Their conduct, he added, in now refusing to give up the cattle showed that they were anything but gentlemen, and he would not treat with them any further, but would take matters into his own hands. He read his answer to the Rangers, and said:

"The cattle are in that pen, over on the other side of the river, near the bank. What shall we do?"

"Go over and take them," answered the boys.

"That's just what I wanted you to say," said the Captain;

"but, as it is a rather risky undertaking with our force, I preferred that the suggestion should come from some of you."

We dismounted and went across the river in the ferry-boat. There were five or six of the Rurales, as many customs officers and about forty regular Mexican soldiers guarding the cattle when we reached the other side of the Rio Grande. These men drew up in line to receive the Rangers, and their commander stepped forward to talk to Captain McNelly. The Captain quickly stated the object of his visit. The Mexican officer said he had no orders to deliver the cattle that day, and the chief customs officer said export duties would have to be paid by us before he could let the cattle go.

This kind of talk did not in the least improve McNelly's temper, and he began chewing on the end of a cigar, a sure sign that he was excited and dangerous.

"Those cattle are going to be turned over to us now," he said. "As for the claim for duty, there was no duty paid when they were stolen and brought over here and, by the Eternal! there shall be no duty paid now."

It looked very like a fight then, and Armstrong, at a signal from the Captain, gave the command:

"Attention! Load carbines! Ready!"

The effect was ludicrous. As the Rangers brought their guns to their hips, preparatory to taking aim, the Mexican officers threw up their hands and told us to take the cattle as soon as we pleased.

"No," said the Captain, "we don't propose to take them; you'll deliver them properly on the other side. Now, if you damned scoundrels don't turn in and drive those cattle across the river as quickly as possible, we'll shoot every one of you."

The Captain marched us farther from the river, so that we had the men and the herd between us and the water. Then we made the Mexicans undress and swim the cattle across to Texas. In this way, they crossed two hundred and fifty head. We gave a cow to the ferry-man for taking us back, sarcastically thanked the Mexicans for their kind assistance, and went away from the ferry, driving the cattle before us.

The soldiers from Fort Ringgold, who were interested spectators of our movements, cheered us heartily, and the people of Rio Grande City joined in with yells of approval.

Later, we turned over the cattle to their owner, Richard King, the wealthiest ranchman in the West at that time. He sent Captain McNelly a check for $1,500 as a reward, and this was divided up among the men, giving us $50 each.

McNelly's chagrin at the manner in which the United States military authorities failed to back him up in his attempt to destroy one of the most notorious of the raiders' ranches in Mexico took form, about two weeks later, in the following letter, which he wrote when he returned to Brownsville:

BROWNSVILLE, December 2, 1875.

GENERAL WILLIAM STEELE,
Adjutant-General, Austin, Texas.

Sir: The condition of this frontier is pitiable in the extreme. The lives and property of our citizens are entirely at the mercy of the Mexican hordes of robbers that infest the banks of the Rio Grande. The State forces, be they ever so active, can only protect the country in the immediate neighborhood of their camp. The hour the camp is moved, it is known on the opposite bank of the river, and the thieves positively steal stock from the site of the camp before the next night. Then, with scarcely an exception, all the male population of the ranches on the opposite bank, from Matamoras to Piedras Negras, are directly engaged in this cattle-stealing business; and three-fourths of the population of this border, for one hundred miles back, are the beneficiaries of this illicit traffic. So we cannot reasonably expect any very active or efficient assistance from the better-disposed class of people living on the border.

The thieves are getting bolder than ever. For a time, immediately after my arrival, I evidently alarmed them by throwing out hints of the approach of several companies of State troops, and that, on their arrival, these long-time robbers would be dealt with severely; but the troops never came, and now crossing cattle seems to be going on by wholesale.

On November 15th, one hundred and twenty-five head were crossed, one mile below Ringgold Barracks. From the 19th to the 21st, two herds, numbering some four or five hundred in all, were crossed below Brownsville. About the 9th, one herd crossed nine miles below Edinburgh. And so they cross, every full moon. They have done the same thing for the last ten years, and they will continue to do so until the robbers are followed to their fastnesses in Mexico and taught that there is no refuge, even in the land of "God and Liberty," for the perpetrators of such outrages.

The policy pursued so long by our Government, of policing our border so ineffectually that the raiders may cross cattle as they please, must now be admitted by the most obtuse of its stupid originators to be a miserable failure. Criminal I call it, for it has permitted our people to be robbed and impoverished, our men murdered and our women outraged.

Shall this condition of affairs continue? It rests with the authorities of the State to answer, yes or no. Let the Governor make one more demand on the President; and then, in case the Cuban question, or some other *Fish* affair, prevents the President from giving us the protection to which we are entitled under the Constitution of the United States, let the Governor order out the militia of the State to repel these invaders.

Although our State is poor—not yet recovered from the effects of the war—I will warrant that enough men and money can be raised to put a stop to these diabolical outrages, from Texas and by Texans. I, for one, will guarantee to raise one company for ninety days that shall not cost the State one dollar.

This may look like an extraordinary course, but, General, this is an extraordinary condition of affairs. These people are American citizens, Texans. They are being murdered, robbed, driven from their homes; and shall we wait for the political clock to strike the hour for putting a stop to it? When will the hour come? We have waited ten years, and ten long years they have been to the people of this desolated border; and still no signal, no sign of relief. God help our frontiersmen if they have to wait ten years more!

With my present force, I can do but little. These raids are made from seventy-five to one hundred miles from my camp, and by the time I receive information and get to the crossing, the raiders are over the Rio Grande and safe from our men, as at almost any point on the whole line of the river, from Matamoras to Piedras Negras, they can gather from one hundred to two hundred men to resist us if we attempt a crossing. And, now that the regular Mexican cavalry have come from Monterey, it will be much worse, as they are anxious to have revenge for our crossing at Los Cuevos and forcing them to submit to such humiliating terms.

The regular troops tell the thieves that if we ever dare cross again, they will never let one of us return to Texas; but, with two hundred men, I could recapture any herd of cattle they might cross, in spite of raiders or regular troops, and unless this can be done, I would respectfully recommend that this troop be ordered elsewhere, or disbanded. It is too humiliating to follow the thieves to the bank of the river and see our stock on the opposite bank, and have the raiders defy us to cross, but crossing with my present force is almost certain destruction.

I was very much annoyed at all those false reports put out by the Mexican officials of Matamoras about our being surrounded and asking for quarter at Los Cuevos. The idea of Texans asking quarter from robbers, assassins and ravishers! On the contrary, it was *they* who asked for terms, and granted *our* demands, and were happy when we left their side of the river. They admit having twenty-seven killed and nineteen wounded, and our loss was one horse wounded. As one of the boys remarked, "We went over and came back with our heads and backs up."

Very respectfully,

(Signed)   L. H. McNelly.

CHAPTER XIII

RESULT OF THE LOS CUEVOS FIGHT

Despite Captain McNelly's gloomy views, as expressed in the characteristic letter I have given from his pen, the result of the Los Cuevos fight was highly satisfactory to the cattle-men, for the raids practically ceased while we remained on the lower Rio Grande. We had done our work so effectually, indeed, that we were forced to have a very prosaic time for months. We went upon many scouts and did plenty of hard riding, but we seldom got a chance to do any fighting. The Mexicans simply would not resist us. If we wanted any of them for past offenses, all we had to do was to find them, and they submitted to arrest with painful humility. They seemed completely cowed.

The border was quieter than it had been since the independence of Texas was won. Less than fifty young men had done more to enforce order on the Rio Grande than thousands of the United States troops had been able to do in years. Tireless riding, deadly shooting, and utter disregard for danger caused the Rangers to be dreaded by evil-doers, far and wide. The good people of the frontier, the hardy settlers and cattle-men, were loud in their praises of us, and the wealthy ranch-men vied with each other in rewarding us for recovering stock.

But the Rangers were not pleased. The quieter life was entirely too tame for us. We had had so much exciting adventure that the habit had grown on us. The routine of camp life was not to our taste. We wanted a chance again to do active work at the mechanical end of a carbine. Shooting blue quail and wild turkeys around camp was good enough exercise in its way, but the blue quail and the turkeys couldn't shoot back, and the exciting element of danger was missing. Solitaire is a dull game, after poker.

Speaking of poker, reminds me that the Rangers were, one and all, inveterate poker-players, and the money we received for recovered cattle, and which was equally divided among the men, was ever changing hands. So was it with our pay of $40 a month. In a day or two after pay day, it was not unusual for four or five of the more lucky ones to have about all the money in camp, the rest of the boys going without funds, or borrowing until pay day came around again. I was never one of the lucky ones and was "flat broke" for months at a time, while some of the successful fellows were squandering my pay.

Captain McNelly did not approve of the gambling, and one day he sent word from Brownsville that he would discharge any man who played poker thereafter. A week later, we sent him a round-robin, in which we stated that all the signers were confirmed poker-players. It was signed by every member of the company, excepting the commissioned officers. As we expected, we never heard anything further from Captain McNelly about the gambling, for he had been at too much pains to select his men to think of discharging all of them for such an offense.

We practised shooting a great deal and bet on our marksmanship contests. The men were nearly all remarkably fine shots, both with their carbines and six-shooters. One of our favorite methods of practising was to ride at a full run past a tree and try to put all six shots from a revolver into it as we sped by. We also spent much time in practising the gentle Texas art of "drawing a gun" quickly from its holster. It isn't the best shot who comes out ahead always in an impromptu frontier duel; it is the man who gets his six-shooter out and in action first.

One of our most popular forms of amusement was playing practical jokes on each other, and some of them were of a pretty rough character. I remember one joke we played on Rector, a jolly and useful member of the troop, albeit so deaf one had to yell at him to make him hear. The boys called him "Reck." He was fond of natural history, and was never so delighted as when he captured a curious insect, or shot a rare bird, or killed a fine specimen of a snake. One day, one of the boys asked Reck if he'd ever gone "sniping."

"Shooting snipe?" said Reck. "Lots of times."

"No, no," said the Ranger, "not shooting them; catching them in a bag. I thought nearly everyone knew about 'sniping.'"

"Never heard of it," said Reck. "How can anyone catch snipe in a bag?"

"Oh, it's simple enough when you know how," explained the other. "A party of half a dozen or more men start out about sundown and go to some marshy place, near a river, where the snipe are apt to be at night. They take a bag—an old gunny-sack is best—and some candles with them. They select a likely spot and, when it is quite dark, one of the party holds the mouth of the bag open and places a lighted candle in front of it, on the ground. The others go off and make a big circle, which they gradually narrow as they approach the one who is holding the bag. They beat the chaparral and make all the noise they can as they get near to him, and they frighten all the snipe and start them running toward him, too. The snipe are attracted by the light from the candle and, as they get close to it, are blinded by its rays. They run straight into the mouth of the open sack. It's great sport, and I know a place, about three miles from here, where the snipe are as thick as hops. Let's get up a party to go after them to-night."

Reck was delighted with the idea and a party of nine snipe-hunters was quickly made up. Strangely enough, all of the men except Reck had often been on sniping expeditions and knew all about them. I was in the secret and formed one of the party.

We started soon after sundown and went up the river, led by the Ranger who proposed the sport. He took us, by winding, roundabout paths, to a swampy piece of ground where we sank to our ankles at every step. The place was swarming with mosquitoes. When we reached what we agreed was a favorable spot, we stopped and had an animated discussion as to who should hold the sack. We all wanted to hold it apparently, because it was so much more fun to bag the snipe than to go tramping around in the brush, beating up the birds. Finally someone said that it took more skill to beat up the snipe than it did to hold the sack and, as Reck was green at the work, perhaps it would be better to let him have the coveted part. The rest agreed to this as a fair solution of the question and two candles were lighted and stuck in the marshy ground, while Reck squatted down and held the mouth of the sack open behind them. It took both his hands to hold the sack properly, and when we left him the mosquitoes were singing in high glee about his head.

And so we came away from him. To beat up the snipe? Oh, no; to go, by the nearest way, out of that mosquito-infested marsh and back to camp. We reached there shortly, and the boys howled with wicked delight as we drew graphic pictures of poor Reck holding on with both hands to that sack, while every mosquito in the swamp within sight of the candles made a bee line for the spot.

Reck came into camp about midnight. He got lost in hunting
it and came near having to pass the night in the brush. He
brought the sack with him and went straight to where the man
who had invited him to go "sniping" lay asleep. He woke him
up and all near him with a wild warwhoop.

"Hello, Reck!" exclaimed the practical joker, as he sat up;
"did you get any snipe?"

"You bet your boots I did!" cried Reck, as he suddenly shook
the contents of his sack all over the joker. "Look at all those fine
fellows."

The man gave a yell and scrambled to his feet. Reck had
shaken about two quarts of big black ants all over him, and he
knew from experience that ants in Texas bite like fiends. Reck
had stumbled over an ant-hill in wandering back to camp and
gathered a lot of them into his sack, so as to get even with the
sniping party. He did it very effectually, for the ants spread in
all directions and made things decidedly uncomfortable for us the
rest of the night. That was the last "sniping" party we ever had
in the Rangers, but it was far from being the last practical joke
played. I invented one myself and worked it with wonderful
success for a long time before I was found out.

I discovered, one day, quite by accident, that I could perfectly
imitate the peculiar trilling hiss of the rattlesnake. This I believe
to be a unique accomplishment; at least, I have never met anyone
who could do it. The sound is made by a trilling tongue-movement
and a hiss. The first time I tried it was one day while riding
quietly along the road from Brownsville to our camp. It must
have been a very fine imitation of the rattlesnake, even at that
first attempt, for my horse gave a great leap and nearly unseated
me, as he shied off about ten feet to one side. That set me to
thinking, and I felt that if I could deceive a horse with the imitation, it would be a simple matter to fool a man. Having so reasoned, I practiced for awhile and waited until evening.

When we had all "turned in," except the one Ranger who stood
the first two hours' guard duty, I thought it time to try the effect
of my new accomplishment on the boys. Some of them were
asleep, but most were awake. I began to hiss very softly, as I lay
on my blanket, and gradually increased the volume of the sound,
until it seemed as if a very angry rattler must be close by. Four
or five of the men sat bolt upright and listened. I waited for

a few minutes, and then "rattled" again. This time more of the men sat up and, to avoid suspicion, I did likewise.

I kept on hissing and the excitement in the camp grew. Two or three jumped up and pulled on their boots, and I did the same. We began a cautious hunt for the rattlesnake, and whenever I was far enough away from the others I started the rattling again. In a short time the entire camp was in commotion. We hunted the elusive snake for nearly an hour, and most of the boys sat up for an hour or two longer after it ceased to rattle, for I stopped after awhile and went to sleep.

I played this interesting little game four nights in succession before I was caught at it. Then the boys entered into a conspiracy to keep me awake. For two nights, whenever I tried to sleep, they got around me and woke me up. They relieved each other at the work. The third night I took a blanket, slipped off into the chaparral and slept about half a mile from the camp.

If any of the boys attempted to take a *siesta* in the afternoon, as was quite natural in the lazy life about camp, he had a miserable time of it. One favorite way of awakening a sleeper was to run close by his head, dragging a saddle over the ground and shouting "Whoa!" at the tops of our voices. The sleeping man would think a horse was running away close to him and would invariably start up in alarm. I have seen a man awakened in this way twice within an hour, and he was every bit as frightened the second time as the first. It was impossible to get used to waking up that way.

Another little pleasantry practiced was for one of the boys to wait until a number of the others were comfortably disposed around the camp-fire after supper, and then approach and toss a few pistol or carbine cartridges into the fire. The resulting scramble to get away from the fire was always a source of pure delight to the cartridge thrower. We became used to this after awhile, however, and would rake the cartridges out of the fire and keep them. We learned that a cartridge will not explode under such circumstances for a minute or two, and so we rescued them for better use.

The above are but a few of the thousand and one practical jokes which the Rangers in McNelly's command were ever perpetrating. We were boys, not only in appearance, but in our amusements as well. I do not remember any instance where practical joking led to bad feeling between the joker and his victim. Reckless and daring though they were, ever ready to jump into the middle of a fight against a common enemy, the Rangers seldom or never quarrelled among themselves. We were like a great band of brothers, and our affection for each other was genuine. There was not an unpopular man in the troop. All were received into the common brotherhood. There was no back-biting, there were no petty jealousies. Unlike most practical jokers, each man was willing to be occasionally a victim himself to the sport of the others, or, if not exactly willing, he never openly objected.

There was one other good reason for treating practical jokes in a good-natured way; every man realized that a fight with any one of his fellows would mean a duel to the death. I don't believe any knew the A B C of "the noble art of self-defense" with nature's weapons. Our only weapons of offense or defense were those which worked with a trigger.

CHAPTER XIV

CAPTURE OF KING FISHER AND HIS BAND

The memory of the camp life on the lower Rio Grande is a pleasant one to me, but it is hardly of such a character as to furnish material for a story of adventure, so, without lingering, I shall pass over the time which intervened between our big raid into Mexico and the day when orders came for us to remove our camp permanently to another portion of Texas. We had done all that was possible with our small force to subdue the border thieves, and Captain McNelly was of too active a temperament to be content to rest quietly while there was work to do in other places.

The American desperadoes were swarming all over Western Texas, and the Sheriffs in many counties were powerless to do anything toward their suppression. The Captain decided that the time had come for us to take an active part in the problem of restoring order in those counties which were overridden and terrorized by fugitives from justice of nearly every State in the Union. So, one day, the welcome order came for us to move camp and we started on a long ride up the Rio Grande.

We travelled slowly—not more than twenty-five miles a day— and we went as straight as possible to Laredo. My feelings upon riding into that town were very different from those with which I had last ridden out of it. Almost the first man I met was Gregorio Gonzales, the City Marshal. He treated me with marked deference, which, I regret to say, I returned with scant courtesy. I was not so ready to pass politely over old scores as he seemed to be.

It was May 25, 1876, when we arrived at Laredo, and we camped near the town for three days. Then we continued our journey on toward the Nueces River, where we camped not far from the place where I had helped Peterson lay out homestead sections, over a year before. Here we remained for a few days to rest our horses, and then began our work of running desperadoes to earth—the work which has made Western Texas a law-abiding, safe country in which to live.

At the camp near the Nueces, we learned first about the desperado, King Fisher, and his notorious gang of horse-thieves, cattle-thieves, and murderers. Fisher lived on the Pendencia Creek, near the Nueces, in Dimmit County. He had a little ranch there, and about forty or fifty of his followers were nearly always with him. These men, too lazy or too vicious to work for themselves, preyed upon the substance of the toiling settlers. They stole the ranchmen's horses and cattle and robbed their corn-cribs, and they did not stop at murder to further their ends. Captain McNelly (I was then his field secretary) wrote, in a letter to the Adjutant-General, from this part of Texas:

"You can scarcely realize the true condition of this section, from Oakville to this point. The country is under a perfect reign of terror from the number and desperate character of the thieves who infest this region. The country is rich in stock, but very sparsely settled, and the opportunities and inducements to steal are very great.

"This county (Dimmit) is unorganized and is attached to Maverick County for judicial purposes. About one-half the white citizens of Eagle Pass are friends of King Fisher's gang. The remainder of the citizens there are too much afraid of the desperadoes to give any assistance in even keeping them secure after they have been placed in jail, and they would never think of helping to arrest any of them. On my arrival there, I found the people greatly terrified, and on the eve of deserting their homes and property to save their lives—the homes which for years they had defended against Indians and Mexicans alternately, and never once thought of leaving. Some of the oldest and best citizens told me that, in all of their frontier experience, they had never suffered so much as from these white robbers. For weeks past they have not dared to leave their homes for fear of being waylaid and murdered.

"Every house in this part of the county has been repeatedly fired into by armed men, from fifteen to twenty in number at a time. The ranchmen's horses and cattle have been driven from their range, and even from pens at the houses, until the people are left almost destitute of means of support. If anyone had the temerity to protest against being robbed, he was told that he had just so many days to live if he did not leave the country. Some of those who had the courage to remain have been foully murdered.

"As the country is so sparsely settled, there are not enough good citizens to defend themselves, even if they united to do so. They seem perfectly willing to assist me, provided the desperadoes are properly secured and tried where they will get justice. They will not get justice here, even if they are brought to trial, which is doubtful. Should they be let off and return here, this country would be in even a worse condition than it is now. No witnesses can be found who will dare to testify against the desperadoes, and I am told by the Circuit Judge that he is convinced no jury in the three counties—Dimmit, Maverick, and Live Oak—can be found to convict them, notwithstanding all their lawless, brutal conduct and the many complaints made against them.

"There is a regularly organized band of the desperadoes, from Goliad to the head-waters of the Nueces, numbering four or five hundred men. The band is made up of men who have committed crimes in different portions of this State and farther east and who have run out here for safety. When they get here they go to robbing for a livelihood. They divide up into parties of twenty-five to forty men and form settlements in the different counties, communicating with each other constantly. They pass the stolen horses along the line continually, and are in communication with other gangs to the north of this place and far to the west."

Some idea of the extent to which the desperadoes swarmed over the western portion of Texas may be obtained when I state that the Rangers had a printed book, containing the names of over three thousand fugitives from justice who were known to be or to have been in that country. And of the three thousand names in the book the large majority were those of men who were "wanted" by the authorities for crimes of the most serious character, such as murder, arson, highway robbery, burglary, and horse and cattle stealing. More than a thousand were murderers, and had rewards on their heads ranging from a few hundreds to ten thousand dollars.

As undoubtedly there were very many desperadoes in the country whose names were not in the book, it will be seen how formidable were their numbers.

To break up the organized bands of these lawless, desperate men, to hunt them down, to arrest them and put them in jail, or to drive them out of the country, was the work we had cut out for us. We had less than fifty men; they had thousands. But we were backed by the law and the good-will of all the honest frontiers-men—a big factor in our favor. And then we made up in self-confidence and reckless disregard of danger what we lacked in numbers. Our success on the lower Rio Grande gave us the feeling that we were invincible. We not only did not fear the result of a conflict with the desperadoes; we were eager to try conclusions with them.

The fourth morning after arriving in camp, we started for the Pendencia, to arrest King Fisher and those of his gang who should happen to be with him. The Captain had received information from some of the less timid ranch-men that Fisher was at his ranch, making ready, they thought, to go on another raid and gather cattle to drive north. These men said that Fisher had about thirty men with him at that time at his place. His house was at Carrizo Springs.

McNelly divided the troop into two squads when we started, and we proceeded in the direction of Fisher's stronghold, the two squads being about two miles apart and travelling in parallel lines. Scouts were sent out about a mile in advance and told to ride half a mile apart and arrest all the men they saw. In this way, a number of men were picked up and turned over to the main troop for safe keeping. We wanted to take Fisher and his gang by surprise, and we did not propose to be thwarted by his friends apprising him of our coming. We went very rapidly, and by unused roads and trails, and succeeded in arriving at a point in the chaparral about a quarter of a mile from Fisher's house without being seen by any of his men.

Both squads came together at this place, but Captain McNelly divided us again and sent part of the troop through the chaparral, around to the other side of the house. Then, at a pre-arranged moment, we all dashed for the house at full speed, six-shooters in hand. A fence was in our way, but the horses went over it like so many hunters after the hounds, and before Fisher and his men perceived us we were within a hundred yards of the place.

Most of the desperadoes were playing poker under the shed-like extension in front of the ranch-house. They jumped up and started for the house proper to procure their arms, but before half of them succeeded in getting inside the door, we were on them and our six-shooters were cocked and pointed at their heads.

"You'll have to surrender or be killed!" cried McNelly to Fisher, who stood half-way out of the door, with the lieutenant of his band, one Burd Obenchain, but known to his companions as Frank Porter.

Fisher did not move, but Porter half raised his Winchester, and coolly looked along the line of Rangers.

"Drop that gun!" yelled McNelly. "Drop it, I say, or I'll kill you."

Porter looked McNelly squarely in the eyes, half raised his rifle again, and then slowly dropped it to his side, and with a sigh leaned it against the side of the house.

"I reckon there's too many of yer to tackle," he said, calmly. "I only wisht I'd a-seen yer sooner."

The other men gave up without a struggle. They were badly frightened at first, for they thought we were members of a vigilance committee, come to deal out swift justice to them and hang them by lynch law. They were agreeably disappointed when they discovered we were the Rangers, officers of the law of Texas.

There were only nine of the desperadoes at the house at the time, but a precious gang of outlaws and cut-throats they were. Here are their names: J. K. Fisher, known as "King" Fisher; Burd Obenchain, alias Frank Porter, wanted for murder and cattle-stealing, as desperate a ruffian as ever the Texas border knew; Warren Allen, who shot a negro in a bar-room at Fort Clark for drinking, at the same bar with him, and then deliberately turned and finished his own drink and ordered another; Bill Templeton, horse-thief; Al Roberts, Will Wainwright, Jim Honeycutt, Wes Bruton, and Bill Bruton. All of them were "wanted" for numberless crimes. They were the head men of the gang of murderers and all-round criminals.

Porter had followed a man all the way from Kansas to Southwest Texas to kill him. He rode up to where his enemy had camped one evening and dismounted.

"Howdy," said the man.

"I haven't seen yer fur some time; how're yer gettin' along?" said Porter.

"Pretty so-so," said the man. "How're you doin'?"

"Only tol'ble," said Porter; "I'm plumb wore out, ridin' an' campin' on yer trail. I reckon yer know what I've come fur?"

"Yes," said the man, "I reckon I do. Ain't yer goin' to gi' me no chanst?"

"Nary chanst," said Porter; "I'm a-goin' to kill yer right where yer be, but I ain't in no hurry ef yer don't move fur yer gun. Le's have supper first; I wanter talk to yer."

Then this villain calmly ate his supper at the man's camp-fire, and, after he finished it, deliberately shot and killed his host.

A few weeks before we arrested them, King Fisher and Frank Porter, by themselves, stole a herd of cattle from eight Mexican *vaqueros* who were driving the herd for its owner, near Eagle Pass. Fisher and Porter rode around the herd and killed every one of the eight Mexicans. The *vaqueros* were all buried together, and the place where they were buried was known as "Frank Porter's Graveyard." I saw it afterward.

Fisher had the reputation of having killed twelve men—"not counting Mexicans." I am quite serious in writing this. The taking of a Mexican's life by the white desperadoes was of so little importance in their eyes that they actually didn't count such an "incident" in their list of "killings," as the murders were styled by them. Only white victims were reckoned by notches on their six-shooters. A glance at the handle of a "bad man's" six-shooter was sufficient to determine how many men he had murdered, as he kept tally by cutting a little notch for each life taken.

Fisher was about twenty-five years old at that time, and the most perfect specimen of a frontier dandy and desperado I ever met. He was tall, beautifully proportioned, and exceedingly handsome. He wore the finest clothing procurable, but all of the picturesque, border, dime-novel kind. His broad-brimmed white Mexican *sombrero* was profusely ornamented with gold and silver lace and had a golden snake for a band. His fine buckskin Mexican short jacket was heavily embroidered with gold. His shirt was of the finest and thinnest linen and was worn open at the throat, with a silk handkerchief knotted loosely about the wide collar. A brilliant crimson silk sash was wound about his waist, and his legs were hidden by a wonderful pair of *chaparejos,* or "chaps," as the cow-boys called them—leather breeches, to protect the legs while riding through the brush. These *chaparejos* were made of the skin of a royal Bengal tiger and ornamented down the seams with gold and buckskin fringe. The tiger's skin had been procured by Fisher at a circus in Northern Texas. He and some of his fellows had literally captured the circus, killed the tiger and skinned it, just because the desperado chief fancied he'd like to have a pair of tiger-skin "chaps." His boots were of the finest high-heeled variety, such as cow-boys love to wear. Hanging from his cartridge-filled belt were two ivory-handled, silver-plated six-shooters. His spurs were of silver and ornamented with little silver bells.

He was an expert revolver-shot, and could handle his six-shooters quite as well with his left hand as with his right. He was a fine rider, and rode the best horses he could steal in Texas or Mexico. Among the desperadoes, the stolen horses were known as "wet stock"—*i. e.,* horses which had been stolen in Mexico and swum across the Rio Grande to Texas, or *vice versa.*

We took the men with us at once to Eagle Pass and put them in jail there. We tied the feet of the prisoners to their saddle-stirrups and then tied the stirrups together under the horses' bellies. We also tied the desperadoes' hands to the pommels of their saddles and led their horses. Before we started, Captain McNelly told us, in the hearing of the prisoners and of Fisher's wife—a pretty girl, with wonderfully fine, bold black eyes—that if any of our prisoners attempted to escape, or if an attempt was made to rescue them, we were to kill them without warning or mercy. That is, or was, known on the frontier as *la ley de fuga,* the shooting of escaping or resisting prisoners. It was well understood among the outlaws, and was a great protection to the officers who were compelled to carry prisoners for long distances over the sparsely settled country. The knowledge of this rule of the border prevented members of a desperado gang from attempting to rescue prisoners, for such an attempt meant instant death to the captives.

It was about forty miles, in a westerly direction, from Carrizo Springs to Eagle Pass, the county seat of Maverick County, situated on the Rio Grande, directly opposite the Mexican town of Piedras Negras, now called Ciudad Porfirio Diaz. Only a part of the Ranger troop went with the prisoners; the others, including Captain McNelly, went into camp, and scouting parties were sent out in various directions to try and capture other members of King Fisher's gang. As soon as the prisoners were turned over to the Sheriff of Maverick County and put in the little jail in Eagle Pass, the Rangers who had guarded them returned to Carrizo Springs.

Two days later, while we were on our way to Eagle Pass with more prisoners, we met King Fisher and his men returning to Carrizo Springs. They were out on bail, although charged with murder and many other serious crimes. Fisher calmly told Captain McNelly that he was out under $20,000 bail, and that any member of his gang could get all the bail he wanted at any time.

"Very well," said McNelly, "if the people of this section want such men as you running over their country and stealing and murdering, they are welcome. There is no use in working my men night and day for such a farce as this. Turn the prisoners loose, boys."

We untied the bonds of our new prisoners and let them go. Afterwards, we learned that Fisher had sent some of his friends around to the merchants and wealthier citizens of Eagle Pass with the message that he wanted them to go bail for him and the other prisoners in the jail. The merchants well knew that if they refused Fisher's "request" they would probably be robbed and murdered, and so they hastened to do as he wished. A scared justice of the peace and a timorous sheriff made the arrangements for giving the bonds and the men were quickly freed, to continue their work of terrorizing the country where they had for so long held sway.

McNelly was not through with the desperadoes of Fisher's band, but he knew that he would have to deal with them in another way and at another time, and he wisely concluded to draw off his forces and so give them a feeling of security which later would bring trouble upon them.

"If we ever come up here again, we'll come to kill," was all the Captain said to Fisher. "If you keep up your system of robbery and murder, you'll hear from us."

Fisher laughed, and said he would be delighted to see the Rangers at any time and entertain them to the best of his ability. Then we came away.

Chapter XV

WOMEN ARMED WITH DERRINGERS

We struck out across the country toward the southeast and made many arrests, here and there, in La Salle, McMullin, and Live Oak counties, and also in Frio and Atascosa counties. Most of the men we arrested were fugitives from justice from other parts of the State, and we were constantly employed taking them to the county-seats, where they were turned over to the sheriffs for safekeeping until officers from the counties where they were wanted came for them. All this section of Texas was in a lawless state, and I remember that, in Atascosa County alone, there was a murder nearly every day. Men were waylaid on the roads and shot down, or murdered in their homes by assassins shooting at them through the windows.

Every man went armed. A woman buying calico or groceries in one of the country stores was waited upon by a clerk who had a six-shooter dangling from his belt. School teachers carried their guns with them to the school-houses. Ministers—parsons they were called, as a rule—went armed to church and preached to armed congregations. Men looked carefully to the placing within easy reach of their revolvers, rifles, or shot-guns before retiring for the night.

Even women carried derringers in many parts of the country, particularly the wives of ranch-men. When the husbands were away from the ranches, the women knew that their best protectors were those provided with easy-working triggers. The country was "on the shoot," to use a colloquial bit of slang, and the six-shooter was the supreme arbiter of most disputes. Little boys were taught to handle and fire pistols and rifles with accuracy, long before they were taught the alphabet.

I wish to emphasize the fact here that, with the passing of the desperado from Texas, the necessity for going armed disappeared, and at this time no man, except he be an officer of the law, or a wild and quarrel-seeking cowboy, thinks it requisite to "tote a gun." More pistols are caried now by men in New York

City than in Texas. Life is as safe in the Lone Star State as it is in the metropolis of America, and all old Texans will bear me out in saying that the Rangers made it so.

We went on to Oakville and made our camp there, scouting in squads throughout Live Oak and the adjoining counties, and making many arrests of men who were "wanted." There was no difficulty in finding them, or in arresting them when found, for already they were beginning in that part of the country to have a wholesome respect for the Rangers, with their ever-ready six-shooters. The outlaws had long laughed the sheriffs and their deputies to scorn, but they found in the Rangers a wholly new force, with which it was not so easy to deal.

We put in several months at this work, and it was while we were in camp at Oakville that Jesse Lee Hall joined the troop as Second Lieutenant, having been appointed to that office by the Governor. Hall succeeded McNelly to the command of the troop in the following year, when McNelly died, and he became one of the greatest terrors to evildoers ever known in the Southwest.

Jesse Lee Hall was born in Lexington, N. C., in October, 1849. He came of old Revolutionary stock by both his parents. His ancestors had settled in North Carolina in the early part of the eighteenth century, coming from the northern English colonies, where their forefathers had lived since early in the seventeenth century. Among Hall's ancestors were the famous General Giles Mebane, and Governor Stanford, of North Carolina.

Hall went to Texas when he was twenty years old, and shortly after became a deputy sheriff in Grayson county, on the line of the Indian Territory, where he did such good work that his fame as an officer attracted wide attention. In the winter of 1876, Hall was appointed Sergeant-at-Arms of the lower house of the Texas Legislature, and so became well acquainted with Governor Hubbard. His appointment to the lieutenancy of the Rangers followed.

I shall never forget the afternoon he first rode into our camp, just below Oakville. We had heard that he was coming and that he was a hard man to deal with, but we soon discovered that he was a splendid fellow, full of fun, of charming manners, and only "nasty" when dealing with outlaws. His hair was bright red, and he soon got the nickname of "Red Hall," which clung to him ever after. When he rode into our camp that afternoon, early in August, 1876, the first thing he did was to sing out:

"Say, have any of you boys got a chew of tobacco? I'm Hall."

We liked that, and we invited him to get down and have something to eat. He did so. Then we beguiled him into telling us some stories of his life as Sergeant-at-Arms at the State capitol. We didn't want to hear the stories so much, but we did want to have a little fun with our new lieutenant. We had it. When he began telling the stories he had an audience of about thirty Rangers. Pretty soon, one of the boys got up and went away. Then another rose and quietly moved off. Then a third stole from the circle. In two minutes, Lieutenant Hall was telling his yarns to the camp-fire, all by himself.

He stopped, and the boys howled in sheer delight at his discomfiture.

"You're a tough lot," said Hall, with a grin.

I think it was while we were camped at Oakville that I had a little turkey-shooting adventure which caused much hilarity in the camp. I had been off hunting some horses which had strayed away from our range and was returning to camp, not having found them. Suddenly, I heard the gobble of a turkey, off to one side, in the mesquite chaparral. The country was full of wild turkeys and quail, and they made a welcome addition to the ordinary camp fare.

As soon as I heard the turkey, I slipped from the saddle, pulled my carbine from its scabbard under the stirrup-leather and crept off into the chaparral. I had not gone far when I spied the big turkey-gobbler with half a dozen turkey-hens. I took very deliberate aim at him and fired. The gobbler fell over and fluttered about on the ground for a minute, but I rushed up and grabbed him and wrung his neck.

He was a gigantic bird, and I felt good as I carried him back to where my horse was standing and tied him to the saddle. I was just tying the last knot when I heard a shout. I turned my head and saw, not twenty yards away, a ranch fence which I had not noticed before. A man was coming toward me, shouting and gesticulating wildly. In a second, I realized the situation. I had shot his tame turkey-gobbler. Wild turkeys and tame turkeys look very much alike, particularly when they are running in the brush, and the mistake was a natural one. But I didn't believe I could explain it to the owner's satisfaction at that time. He didn't look as if he was amenable to reason. He was swearing like a trooper and saying unkind things. I hadn't a cent to pay him for his turkey and I didn't want to fight him for it.

So I waved my hand in a careless, happy farewell to him and started off on a gallop, the turkey flopping up and down behind me in great style.

When I reached camp, I flung the turkey off and the boys began plucking it in a hurry. They wanted to cook it for supper. No one seemed to notice that it wasn't a wild turkey and I didn't enlighten them as to its domesticity.

We fried the turkey and were eating it in full enjoyment of its lusciousness, when my friend, its former owner, rode into camp.

"Which one o' you fellers shot my turkey?" he called out from the saddle.

"Get down and have some supper," answered Durham, who grasped the situation instantly.

"I don't want no supper; I want the man who shot my turkey."

"You must have come to the wrong place, friend," said Durham. "No one here has shot your turkey. I haven't seen a turkey in a month. Any of you boys seen a turkey around here?"

Durham held a leg of the turkey in his hand as he put the question. The boys all answered in the negative, with their mouths full of turkey.

"Why, doggone ye," said the farmer, "you're eatin' my turkey, right now!"

"You are mistaken, sir," said Horace Rowe, carefully picking a wing of the bird; "this is a *meleagris americana* which we are devouring, and we beg that you will accept of our poor hospitality and join us in getting away with it."

This display of learning seemed to stagger the farmer. He dismounted and sat down on the ground with us. Soon he was eating a piece of the turkey. He picked some of the feathers up and carefully examined them.

"That was my turkey all right," he said, gravely.

"Very well," I put in, "if one of the boys really did shoot your turkey, you point him out and we'll arrest him and take him to the justice of the peace in Oakville."

"Yes; pick him out, pick him out!" cried the others.

The man looked all around at the faces and finally picked out Rector.

Rector proved an alibi by half the men in camp. Then the farmer pointed out another man; but we said he couldn't go on guessing that way, and he himself agreed it wouldn't be quite fair. At last he gave it up in despair. Then I gave him a dollar, which I borrowed, and he went away satisfied.

But I kept on hearing about that turkey for a long, long time afterward. The Rangers had a pleasing little way of keeping any awkward episode fresh for an unbearable length of time.

In the latter part of August, Hall took eleven men and went in command of them on his first scout as a Ranger officer. He went to Goliad and did the Sheriff's work during the suspension of that officer for malfeasance in office. Hall and his men made about twenty arrests of desperate men on the trip.

Hall also gave assistance to the sheriffs of other counties in quieting disturbances which arose among the cattle-men. Among those he arrested were George McCarty, Wesley Bruton, and them over to the sheriff of Dimmit County, and they were turned loose on straw bail, at the demand of King Fisher. Early in September, Hall and his men were on duty at the session of the District Court in Live Oak County, to keep order.

As I was not with Hall I cannot give anything but a bare record, in a general way, of his work at this time; but that it was good and showed him to be a fearless and efficient officer there can be no doubt, for, at a later date, I had an opportunity to see him under circumstances to try the nerves of the bravest man, and he was chillingly cool then.

Those of us who were left in camp at Oakville grew very tired of our life there, for it was anything but active. Most of my time was put in herding horses. I remember that I stampeded them one afternoon by shooting at an antelope, and a weary hunt I had before I got them together again.

Early in September, we received word that a Mexican had been murdered near a sheep-corral about twelve miles from camp. Sergeant Orrell took six or seven of us with him to investigate the matter. We arrived at the corral after dark and camped for the night. The weather was insufferably hot, and I could not sleep for a long time. It was not only the heat which kept me awake, but a horrible odor which came from I didn't know where. At last I fell asleep and dreamed of ghastly forms and blood-curdling adventures. I awoke, utterly unrefreshed, at dawn. I looked about me, and there, not six feet from where I lay, was the body of the murdered Mexican.

I had slept with that grewsome thing almost within arm's

reach all night. He had been shot in twenty places and presented a terrible appearance, for the body had lain in the hot sun all the afternoon. My breakfast was limited strictly to black coffee that morning. We never succeeded in catching the murderers of the man. They escaped to Mexico.

Chapter XVI

TWO HUNDRED SHOTS IN FOUR MINUTES

Late in September, Sergeant Armstrong told us, one afternoon, that we were to go on a long and important scout with him— McNelly had gone to San Antonio, sick—and he added, "I believe we'll be lucky enough to have a fight before we get through."

He was right. We not only had the fight, but we succeeded in breaking at last the reign of terror which King Fisher and his gang had established.

It was raining the morning we left camp, twenty-five strong, and started by an old, unused trail up the Nueces River. All day long the rain poured down in torrents, wetting us to the skin. I remember how, after emptying the water out of my pistol holster two or three times, I cut the end of the holster off, so that it would not hold water.

When we camped that night it was hard work to start the camp-fires, for everything in the way of fuel was soaked. Our plan under such circumstances was to get a piece of dead wood and split it so as to get the dry core. This we cut up fine and so started a little blaze which had to be carefully nursed until, by gradually adding larger and larger pieces, enough of a fire was under way to receive wet sticks and dry them.

I lay in two or three inches of water that night, on the ground, and protected my face with my hat to keep the cold rain-drops from hitting it. My clothes and blankets were wringing wet, but so were those of every man in the party. The next day the rain continued as hard as ever, and so it was for the ten days we were on the march up the Nueces. There was not a minute that it cleared off. The river, which ordinarily was a small enough stream, was so swollen that it was three or four miles wide in places. Every night we lay in the rain and every morning we started out again to ride in it.

In any other country, the sick-list would doubtless have been a large one under such conditions, but the Rangers suffered no ill effects from the continuous drenching. Horace Rowe, who was inclined to be consumptive, improved wonderfully in health on the trip and gained in weight. The spirits of the men never lagged for a moment. We were all as happy as so many ducks in a mud-puddle, and more practical jokes were played than there is room to tell about. I remember, one evening, two of the men and I hunted for an hour for a fictitious shepherd's hut to sleep in, carrying our blankets with us through the chaparral until we gave it up in despair and lay down on the ground to sleep until morning. The boys had a good laugh at our expense the next day.

All the way up the Nueces we took every man prisoner we met and made him fall in with us. By the time we reached Carrizo Springs we had over a score of these prisoners, but we effectually prevented the news of our advance upon Fisher's stronghold from becoming known, for it was his gang of desperadoes we were after.

On the night of October 1st, we reached a point near Fisher's house, and succeeded in capturing one Noley Key, a member of his gang. I know not what threats Armstrong used to Key, but he at the last willingly acted as our guide. He told Armstrong that Fisher and his men were away from home. We surrounded the settlement and closed in on it, only to find that Key told the truth and that no one was there but the women and children.

But Armstrong did not give up. He took Key aside and drew from him the information that a band of horse-thieves were in camp on the banks of Lake Espintosa, six or seven miles distant. Key told Armstrong that seven men were in the band, and that they had forty or fifty stolen horses which they were going to drive farther north in a few days.

Armstrong immediately divided his men, sending eighteen of the Rangers down to another desperado settlement and taking six with him to go to the lake. The six were Devine, Durham, Evans, Boyd, Parrott, and myself. Key acted as our guide and we started off. The rain had ceased during the afternoon and a full moon was riding high in the heavens.

We rode slowly for about an hour and then turned off into some woods, where we dismounted. Key pointed out the location of the thieves' camp and then was told to remain where he was, with Evans and Devine who were left in the woods in charge of the horses.

"Boys," said Armstrong to the four men who were left with him, "we are going to capture those thieves or kill them. The reason I did not bring more men along was because I was afraid these fellows wouldn't resist us if we were so many. Key tells me that they stood off the Sheriff and his posse a few nights ago, and so they'll be looking for officers and be prepared to fight. That's just what we want. If they will only fire at us, we can rush in on them and kill the last one of them. Nothing but that will break up this gang. I only hope they'll show fight. Now, come along and don't make any noise."

We advanced slowly and cautiously through the brush, and soon came to a wide, open space, near the lake. We looked across the open space and saw the camp-fire of the horse-thieves' camp, but could see no one stirring. Very cautiously, bending down and moving as swiftly as we could in that position, we approached the fire. We were within twenty-five yards of it, when suddenly a figure rose and a yell split the silence.

"Here they come, boys! Here they come!" shouted the man who had arisen. In an instant the seven men at the camp were up and the one who had shouted fired at us.

I heard Armstrong cry, "Damn you, you'll shoot at an officer, will you?" and then the firing grew furious on both sides. We rushed in on them and there was a continual blaze from the firearms.

Just in front of me was a man emptying his six-shooter at me and I raised my carbine and fired at him. The moment before I fired he had his mouth open, yelling curses at me; but with my shot he dropped like a dog. I thought I had killed him and turned my attention to the others, but, except for one man with whom Boyd was having a fierce hand-to-hand fight with knives, all were either dead or had jumped into the lake.

Over and over rolled Boyd and the desperado, but in the end Boyd jerked himself loose, his knife dripping with the thief's heart-blood.

The fight lasted not more than three or four minutes, but in that time fully two hundred shots were fired. We turned over the bodies of the dead men. They were all well-known desperadoes— John Martin, alias "One-eyed John;" "Jim" Roberts, and George Mullen. The man whom I shot was named McAlister. I was bending over and looking at his face, when I saw his eyes move.

"Hello!" I cried; "this man isn't dead."

McAlister looked straight at me and began to beg for his life.

"For God's sake, gentlemen, don't kill me," he begged piteously. "For God's sake don't kill me!"

"No one wants to kill you," I said. "We are not murderers. Would you like some water?"

He murmured that he would, and I took a tin cup from beside the camp-fire and went down to the lake and dipped it full of water. When I returned to him, I put it to his lips and he drank. He told me he was wounded in the leg and a part of his jaw was also shot away. I thought he would surely die, but we promised to send a wagon for him and made him as comfortable as we could before we left him. Then we returned to where we had left our horses with Devine and Evans.

As I was walking silently along in the woods with the rest of the boys, I heard suddenly, close in front of me, the sharp click of a gun being cocked, and the quick demand:

"Halt!"

I stopped so quickly that I nearly fell over backward. It was Devine who gave the command, and in a moment we told who we were. Evans stood close to Devine.

"Where's Noley Key?" asked Armstrong.

"Dead," said Devine.

"Dead?"

"Yes. When he heard the firing, he jumped up and started to run, and we fired at him. One of us killed him, for there's a bullet-hole in his back."

We went over and looked at Key where he lay, face downward. I felt badly about him, for on the way to the camp he had been talking in a pleasant way to me and I had given him some tobacco. He was no great loss to the community, however, for he was a well-known horse-thief.

Before I go on with the record of this night's adventures, I may say that McAlister recovered and, so far as I know, is alive to this day. When I went to Texas, in 1892, he turned up one day in San Antonio and told some men in a bar-room that he was there for the express purpose of killing me.

"I've been camping on his trail for sixteen years," he said; "and now I'm going to kill him for shooting my jaw off that night."

I was told of this, and I lost no time in getting a six-shooter. Then I went on a hunt for McAlister. I thought I should know him, with his disfigured face, a good deal quicker than he would know me, and I relied on the virtue of "the drop," the Texas way of expressing the advantage of being prepared to shoot before the other man is ready.

It got to McAlister's ears that I was after him, and he left town in a hurry. Captain Hall told me afterward that he knocked this same man down one day, a few years before, for using threatening language. I'm afraid Brother McAlister is just a trifle revengeful and ungrateful.

As soon as we mounted our horses again, that night of the fight, we rode over to a ranch, about three miles away, on the banks of the Nueces. We found four men sleeping in the yard of the ranch-house, and awakened them by uncovering them with the muzzles of our carbines. It must be a little alarming to wake up suddenly in the dead of night and find a number of heavily armed strangers yanking the covering from one by the aid of gleaming gun-barrels. If I remember correctly, those men did not look pleased at the proceeding; but they did not protest very loudly. They just lay still and shivered with fright until we told them to get up. We had only been looking under their blankets for arms, so that they would not attempt any resistance, for we had had enough bloodshed for one night. Two of the men Armstrong decided that he wanted, and we made them saddle their horses and go with us. Then we returned to where we had parted from the other squad of Rangers.

Going back along the road, I was on the right hand of one of our prisoners. I believe Boyd was on his other side. We were supposed to guard them, but both Boyd and I went to sleep as we rode. We were completely tired out. Suddenly I was awakened by a confused sound of shouting voices and the rattling of a wagon. For a moment I hadn't the least idea where I was or what the noise could be, and I was panic-stricken. My nerves, after all the shooting, were, I suppose, in a shaky condition, and the sudden awakening was horrible in the extreme.

That I was not alone in experiencing these sensations I discovered later, for nearly every man on that ride was asleep. Our prisoners could have escaped with ease if they had dared. Boyd described his awakening to me that night in a manner more forceful than elegant. He said that for a few seconds he imagined himself in the regions infernal—only he didn't put it in that way exactly.

When we got back to camp we found the other eighteen

Rangers there. They had had a little rumpus, too, and killed a man who resisted arrest. He was Pancho Ruiz, wanted for murder at Corpus Christi. I believe Corporal Rudd was the one who killed Ruiz. We were all so tired out and sleepy after our long march in the rain and excitement which followed it that we slept until late in the afternoon, each man standing guard for twenty minutes at a time. It was difficult for anyone to keep awake even as long as that.

That evening I wrote, with Armstrong, the report of the fight, and we started with three others and our two prisoners to Eagle Pass, some forty miles distant. We had captured about fifty head of stolen horses late in the afternoon, near the thieves' camp, and a lot of cattle. As my horse was tired, I decided to give him a rest and ride one of the stolen horses to Eagle Pass. I picked out a fine, big brown horse and saddled him. Armstrong and the other three men also took stolen horses for the ride, but none as fine in appearance as the one I had.

Alas! it is not always well to judge by appearances. I quickly discovered that my horse was a hard trotter, and under no circumstances would he go in a gallop. All the other horses were galloping, with a motion as easy as the rocking of a cradle, but my old fellow did nothing but trot, and that in a way to almost jolt the teeth from my gums. I stood it as long as I could, and then adopted a plan to save myself from being shaken apart. I would make my horse walk very slowly until the others were far ahead —a mile or so; then I would go on a full run until I caught up with them. By adopting this plan and repeating it over and over again, I made that forty miles with some degree of comfort.

We reached Eagle Pass at daylight and made camp in the wagon-yard of the little hotel. While we were eating our breakfast, two guests of the hotel came out and began talking to us. One of them seemed especially curious to learn our business and all about us. After awhile he turned and said he would go in and get his breakfast.

"Take breakfast with us," said Armstrong, cordially.

"No, thank you; I'll go inside," said the man.

"Better stay and eat with us."

"No; I'm much obliged, but I think I'll go in the hotel."

"I think not, my friend."

"Why not? You're not going to arrest me, I hope: I haven't done anything."

"No," said Armstrong, who was looking through our book of fugitives from justice; "no, we won't arrest you because, you see, you have been under arrest for the last fifteen minutes."

The man's jaw fell and he began to tremble, but he tried to bluster and brave it out.

"This is an outrage," he said. "I'm a travelling man and a guest of this hotel."

"I know you're a travelling man," said Armstrong with a smile. "You've travelled all the way from Missouri on funds you stole from a bank there. I don't think you'll travel much farther south, my friend. You'll do your travelling in the other direction now."

The man grew ashy white, but he saw it would be useless to resist. He was an escaped bank cashier and had been wanted for some months. He was kept in jail in Eagle Pass until officers arrived from Missouri and took him back with them.

Chapter XVII

DRAWING LOTS FOR DANGEROUS SERVICE

That morning Armstrong sent the report by wire to Captain McNelly at San Antonio. I later saw it in the San Antonio *Express* under a big "scare" head. We soon discovered that the news of the Espintosa Lake fight had reached Eagle Pass long before we brought it, and a number of desperadoes of Fisher's gang had gone across the Rio Grande to Piedras Negras as a matter of safety. Armstrong went over the river in the afternoon by himself and did not return until after sunset. He was both excited and elated when he reached us.

"I've found out where those outlaws are," he told us, in a tone of much joy. "They're all big men, too—rewards on every one of them. They go to a little *jacal* every night and play cards. We can steal across the river to-night, about nine o'clock and corral the whole lot while they are playing. If they resist us, we can kill them."

"How many of them are there?" I asked.

"Nine," said Armstrong; "and every one is wanted for murder or horse-stealing."

"How do you propose to get them?"

"Go to their shanty and break in the door. Then we can get them."

"What will they be doing while we are breaking in?"

"Oh, I suppose they'll show fight, of course."

We four Rangers who had come to Eagle Pass with Armstrong exchanged glances. Then we looked at him. Finally Boyd said in a quiet tone:

"John Armstrong, you're a————fool."

He didn't mean to show any disrespect to a superior officer. He simply wanted to give voice to his opinion of the Sergeant's plan. Armstrong seemed hurt.

"I thought," said he, in an injured tone, "you boys would follow me anywhere."

"We will," said Boyd; "you know that. But you're a——— fool, all the same, and you're going to get us all killed."

"Nonsense," said Armstrong, much relieved. "Five Rangers can lick nine of those fellows any day of the week, and you know it. We'll go over to-night about nine o'clock and get them."

"And bring them back here with us, I suppose?"

"Certainly—if we don't have to kill them."

"All right," said the boys; "we're with you."

We had supper and spent some little time in carefully inspecting our arms to see they were in complete order, and at about nine o'clock that night proceeded quietly to the ferry-boat landing and were soon poled across to Mexico. Armstrong led us along the dark streets of the little Mexican town and across a plaza. We halted on the plaza, and our leader told us in a low tone that the desperadoes were in a little house, about half-way down one of the streets which led off from it.

"We'd better go down on the other side of the street from the house," he said, "one or two at a time, and then make a break for it when I give the word. I'll smash in the door with the butt of my carbine, and you fellows pile right in after me. I needn't tell you to shoot to kill if they start to make any trouble."

Armstrong went ahead to show us the way, and we followed at short intervals. When we arrived opposite the house, he silently pointed it out, and then we swiftly moved across the narrow street, carbines in hand, ready to fire at an instant's notice. Without a word, Armstrong lifted his carbine and dealt the door a smashing blow with its butt.

Crash! It flew in and, without a second's pause, we dashed into the room. A smoky lamp on a table, which was covered with a jumble of playing-cards and poker-chips, some rush-bottomed chairs, one overturned on the hard dirt floor, and, more significant than all else, the unmistakable fumes of recently smoked corn-shuck Mexican cigarettes, showed that the room had been occupied but a short time prior to our coming; but when we entered it with such a flourish of arms it was empty, so far as desperadoes were concerned. The birds had flown, doubtless having been warned, in some mysterious way, of our advent.

I don't believe any of us regretted their absence except Armstrong. He was deeply chagrined, for he had counted upon bagging those nine desperadoes, or killing them. I think he would have preferred the latter method of dealing with them. We returned to Texas as soon as we realized our errand was fruitless, and, an hour later, were sound asleep in the wagon-yard of the hotel, one man, of course, standing guard, for we were hardly safe without one.

The next evening, the telegraph operator told Armstrong that a band of desperadoes had gone out on the road to Carrizo Springs, for the purpose of waylaying the Rangers on their way to Eagle Pass. We had made no secret of the fact that the rest of the men were coming to the town, and the telegraph operator said the desperadoes had determined to shoot them from ambush on the road.

"We'll have to warn the boys, and quickly," said Armstrong, when we received this news. "Here, Boyd, Jennings, Mayers, saddle up as fast as you can and ride to the Carrizo. You'll probably meet the boys on the way, as they were to leave this afternoon. I wouldn't take the road if I were you. You know the general direction. Cut across the prairie, and ride like hell!"

In a very few minutes we were on our horses and away. I took a white horse which Armstrong had ridden, for I did not relish that forty miles again on my stolen trotter. It was after sunset when we started, but the moonlight made the country almost as bright as day and we flew over the prairie to warn our comrades of the danger which awaited them. We dashed through the mesquite chaparral and cacti, tore over flower-spangled open spaces, skimmed just under the low-hanging boughs of live-oaks and cottonwood trees, always keeping the road a good quarter of a mile or so to our left and going, as Armstrong suggested, by "general direction."

So, for over two hours we rode, slowing down now and then to let our horses get their wind, and then darting ahead once more. At last we came to the thickly wooded banks of a stream and found that we could not cross it. The banks were very steep and covered with brush and drift-wood in a great tangle.

"There's just one place we can cross this creek," said Boyd, "and that's at the road."

"And that's just where those men will be waiting to do their waylaying," said Mayers.

"We'll have to risk it," I said. "We can't wait here, and we must get across."

We rode back from the creek for a few hundred yards and then went slowly toward the road. When we reached it we tossed a coin

to see who should go first, who second, and who last. It fell to
my lot to go first, but I would willingly have relinquished the
honor. I drew my six-shooter and cocked it; Boyd, who came
next, and Mayers, who was last, followed my example.

"Now," said I, "We'll go for all we're worth through that
place. Shoot at anything you see that moves. One of us may get
through anyhow, for it's so dark in there under the trees we
won't be much of a mark."

I remember regretting very keenly then that I had taken Armstrong's white horse instead of my brown trotter, but it was too
late to remedy matters and I consoled myself by thinking that
even if my horse was shot I might escape.

"Are you ready?" I whispered.

"All right," said Mayers.

"Let her go," said Boyd.

I dug the spurs into my horse, leaned well forward in the
saddle and started on a full run, straight for the ford. Down the
bank and into the blackness I dashed, my pistol held at half-arm
and ready; into the foot or more of inky water I splashed, across
it and up the hill on the other side, Boyd close at my horse's heels
and Mayers following.

Up, up, up! the top of the hill was gained! Hurrah! I was
already tugging at the bridle to slow down my horse, when——

God! right in front of me, drawn across the road, were many
men on horses—waiting, I could see the barrels of their six-
shooters and Winchesters gleaming in the moonlight as they
made ready for the fight. I jerked my horse back on his haunches
and flung myself from the saddle to the ground. In a second,
Boyd and Mayers followed suit. We darted quickly into the
brush at the side of the road, knowing that in that way only could
we escape. It was folly to try to fight all those men.

Bang! Crash! and many bullets whistled over our heads and
close to us, clipping the bushes all around where we lay. Then
came the pounding of scores of hoofs and the men were on us.
I had just raised my six-shooter to fire at the leader of the
desperadoes, when I recognized him. It was Corporal Rudd.

"Rudd! Rudd! Don't shoot!" I shrieked. "Look! I'm Jennings!
We're Rangers!"

My voice carried far and clear and was answered by a whoop
and a series of joyful yells. We were safe.

We rode back along the road to Eagle Pass with the men,

throwing out scouts on either side of the road ahead, but saw no sign of the waylaying party. We concluded that the telegraph operator must have been misinformed, but he said not, later. It may be that the desperadoes did not care to risk the attempt to waylay twenty of McNelly's Rangers, for the fame of our prowess had become mighty throughout that land.

The Rangers remained for two or three days in camp, just outside of Eagle Pass, and then started down the Rio Grande. We only rode about ten miles, however, and then turned back and went close to town. As soon as night fell, some of us stole quietly into the town to see if we could pick up some of the men we wanted. Bill McKinney and I were sent to Bruton's saloon to see if we could run across any of the desperadoes there. We succeeded. We were not in the place two minutes before King Fisher himself walked in.

"Whoopee!" he yelled. "All the Rangers have gone down the river. Everybody come up to the bar and take a drink."

McKinney went to the bar and got on Fisher's right hand and I placed myself at the left of the desperado chieftain. He was pouring out a drink of whiskey for himself when he saw McKinney standing by him and recognized him. He turned to me and looked me over. Then he smiled easily and said:

"Well, gosh durn my chaps; I thought you boys were all down the river, and here you are back again. D'you want me for anything?"

"Yes," I said, "we do."

"All right," said Fisher grunting again.

"Here are my guns. What'll you have to drink."

He unbuckled his belt and gave us his two white-handled six-shooters without a murmur. Then we had the drinks and took him to our camp, and that night went with him and several of the Rangers to a *fandango*. Fisher, as usual, gave bail the next day and was released. He didn't mind being arrested very much; it was so very easy for him to get out of trouble again.

There was another fugitive from justice in the bar-room when we arrested King Fisher, but McKinney didn't know it and I had good reasons for not enlightening him. That man was Bill Thompson, the one who came to my assistance when I was fleeing from the Mexicans of the *fiesta* the first night I was in Nueva Laredo. I recognized him instantly and made myself known to him.

"I suppose I ought to tell who you are," I said, "but I won't.

I want to warn you, however, that your description is in our list, and if you don't get over to Mexico pretty quick you are liable to be taken in."

Thompson thanked me and left the room. I was glad to see him take the hint so quickly, for although I owed him a debt of gratitude, it went against my official conscience to connive at his escape.

In a few days we all started back to Oakville again. Armstrong had heard of some Mexican raiders who were killing cattle for their hides on the Nueces River, near Fort Ewell, and he determined to raid their camp, which was on our way back. We drove the fifty stolen horses we had captured, the main body of the men riding ahead and the horse-herders following, a mile or so behind. We were scattered along the road for a couple of miles as we travelled, riding as we pleased.

One morning Armstrong said we were not very far from the raiders' camp, and he ordered us not to make any more noise than possible, as we might scare the Mexicans off. We had a fashion common to cow-boys, Rangers, and all plains-men, of yelling like wild Indians at times, for nothing at all except to give vent to our exuberant spirits, born of the free, big life of the prairies.

Early that afternoon, I was riding with Adams, a good half mile behind Armstrong and the few Rangers who were ahead with him. A rattlesnake crossed the road in front of us and coiled with an angry rattle. Without any thought of the consequences, or of what Armstrong had said about keeping quiet, I pulled my six-shooter and took a shot at the rattler. I missed him, and Adams fired. Then Durham, Parrott, Devine, and Griffin came galloping up to see what was the matter. They all began shooting at the snake from their horses, and at last somebody succeeded in killing it with a bullet. Then we realized we had disobeyed orders and would get into trouble.

We rode slowly ahead—all but Devine—and presently came to where Armstrong had halted and was waiting for us.

"What was all that shooting back there?" he demanded.

"We were shooting at a snake," said Durham.

"I hope you killed it," said Armstrong, sarcastically.

"We did."

"I'm glad to hear it. You've probably scared off those raiders, who must be camped near here."

He looked sternly at us for a few moments and then added:

"Durham, Adams, Jennings, Griffin, and Parrott, you will report to Corporal Rudd for extra guard-duty for a week."

He had not finished speaking before Devine came galloping up at racing speed, his six-shooter in his hand, excitement written all over his face.

"What's all the shooting about?" he panted, as he reined in his horse. "I thought there must be a fight."

Armstrong looked at Devine narrowly for a second. Then his lips curved in a dry smile and he added:

"Devine, you will also report to Corporal Rudd for extra guard-duty for a week."

Armstrong was not an easy man to fool.

We had lots of fun with that extra guard-duty. We stood the first and last reliefs by turns, but most of the nights we all slept the sleep of the just and took chances. The first of the six culprits to wake up in the morning—we were all early risers—would scramble to his feet and begin pacing about with his carbine, and no one outside of the six knew that a strict guard had not been kept all through the night. We might have been more careful in a country where we were looking for trouble, but we felt safe enough to run the risk there.

We found the raiders' camp, after all, and arrested six men in it. One old Mexican wanted to fight, but a crack on the head with the butt of a six-shooter from one of the men changed his notion.

Devine nearly lost his life on the way back, by swimming across the Nueces River when a freshet was making the stream boom. He swam across to get a boat and was caught in some thorny bushes, locally known as "cat-claws," and nearly drowned.

Chapter XVIII

THE GREAT FEUD BETWEEN THE SUTTONS AND THE TAYLORS

The Rangers went to San Antonio shortly after we arrived at the Oakville camp, and I was detailed to go on a scout commanded by Sergeant Orrell to Gillespie County for the purpose of arresting J. B. Johnson, charged with cattle-stealing. We surrounded Johnson's house one night, broke in the door and arrested him. He had sworn he would not be taken alive. We searched the house to see if any others of his gang were there in hiding. I remember going into a bed-room and approaching the bed cautiously to see who was sleeping there. When about six feet from the bed, I heard a noise almost at my feet and, looking down, saw an enormous dog glaring at me in the uncertain light, and evidently prepared to give battle if I advanced another step. I did not advance, but kept my carbine pointed at the big dog's head and cried out to Johnson to call the animal off, which he did. Two children were asleep in the bed.

We started for San Antonio with our prisoner, but that morning learned that an old man had been murdered in the night, near Fredericksburg, and we rode to his ranch to see if we could be of any assistance in hunting down the murderer. When we reached the ranch we found about two hundred excited Germans there— the county was largely settled by Germans—and they were holding an inquest. The murdered man had been a sort of patriarch of the colony, and all the men gathered there were determined upon avenging his death.

The inquest did not disclose the name of the murderer, but a number of the Germans came to the conclusion that our prisoner, Johnson, was the guilty party. A committee waited upon Sergeant Orrell and informed him they were going to hang Johnson, then and there.

"Oh, you are, are you?" said Orrell. "What do you suppose we'll be doing all that time?"

"What do you mean?" asked the spokesman of the proposed lynching party.

"I mean," said Orrell, "that this man is my prisoner and under my protection. I don't believe he killed the old man, but even if I knew him to be the murderer I wouldn't give him up."

"You'll have to do it," said the German. "You only have four men with you and we have about two hundred. We'll take him from you."

Without a word in answer, Orrell handed a six-shooter to Johnson, who was ashy pale and trembling with fear.

"Here," he said, "you take this and defend yourself, if you have to."

Then, turning to the Germans, the Sergeant said:

"Now, gentlemen, if you care to take that man from us, start right in. But I want to tell you one thing first: before you take him you'll have to kill five of McNelly's Rangers, and if you do kill five of McNelly's Rangers—God help your settlement!"

The Germans knew that Orrell meant every word he said, for there could be no doubting the determination of his tone and manner. They also knew that if they killed us—or even one of us—there would come a fearful day of reckoning when our comrades heard the story. They drew off and consulted together, and came to the conclusion that they would not have a lynching-bee that afternoon.

Shortly after, we rode away; Johnson, with a Ranger on either side of him, two Rangers ahead, and Orrell coming behind as a rear guard. We landed Johnson in jail in San Antonio, and he was soon tried for cattle-stealing and sent to the penitentiary at Huntsville.

For the next month or so the Rangers went on short scouting trips and made many important arrests of outlaws. Squads of men were riding here and there over the country, turning up when least expected and terrorizing desperadoes, just as the desperadoes had for years terrorized the settlers. Lieutenant Hall was doing great work in Karnes County. There he arrested eleven of a gang of bank-robbers, and many men charged with cattle-stealing, horse-stealing, and murder.

December 7th, Sergeant Armstrong and J. W. Deggs went in a buggy from the San Antonio camp to arrest John Mayfield, at a ranch about twelve miles distant, for a murder committed in Parker County. Mayfield had sworn he would never give up, but would die before submitting to arrest. So many desperadoes had made this same boast and then had given up quietly that neither

Armstrong nor Deggs expected any trouble in taking Mayfield.

They found the man in a corral near his house. He was break-ing in a colt. Before Mayfield saw them, both Armstrong and Deggs had him covered with their six-shooters. Then Armstrong called out:

"You are under arrest; we are Rangers."

Mayfield turned quickly and looked at the two men.

"Throw up your hands!" commanded Armstrong.

"I'll see you in——first!" shouted Mayfield, pulling his six-shooter and firing at Armstrong.

Just before he shot, Deggs fired and struck Mayfield on his pistol-arm, thus saving Armstrong's life. Mayfield fell, dropping his pistol. He immediately picked it up with his left hand and fired at Deggs, but this time Armstrong shot him and he fell dead, cocking his six-shooter with the last bit of strength he had.

The shooting aroused the settlement around Mayfield's place, and the two Rangers saw men coming from every direction with their guns. They knew that Mayfield had many friends, and they consequently thought discretion the better part of valor, jumped into their buggy, and drove quickly away, arriving at our camp two hours later. Lieutenant Wright and ten men immediately started back with Armstrong and Deggs for the scene of the shooting, but when we arrived there we found that Mayfield's body had been taken away and buried. No one could be found who would tell us where the murderer was buried, although we very much wanted to know. There was a reward of four thousand dollars on Mayfield, dead or alive, but it was never collected, for we could not produce the body.

A few days after this occurrence, I was sent with a number of the men to join Lieutenant Hall's detachment at Clinton, De-Witt County, where a state of great lawlessness had existed for many years.

DeWitt County was notorious for a feud which for over a quarter of a century had existed there between the Taylor and Sutton factions. The Taylor-Sutton feud began back in the '40s, in Georgia, removed to Texas with the opposing families, and was flourishing at the time of which I write, 1876. No vendetta of Corsica was ever carried on with more bitterness than was this feud in Texas. Scores of men had been murdered, nay, hundreds, on both sides, and still the war kept up. Every man in the county had to choose sides in the feud. A new settler was anxiously watched to see which faction he would choose as his. Every man went armed to the teeth. Midnight murders were of frequent occurrence. Waylaying on the roads was considered the correct thing and shooting from ambush was taken as a matter of course.

Matters quieted down a little in the few years preceding 1876, but in the twelve months immediately before the Rangers' advent the feud raged more desperately than ever. There were over a hundred and fifty indictments for murder in the Sheriff's office which had never been acted upon.

Hall had been carefully getting at the facts for some time, and when he sent for reinforcements was all ready to act. He made up his mind to break up the feud and restore order in DeWitt County.

It was a tremendous undertaking, but Lee Hall had perfect faith in his ability to carry it through successfully. I know of no better illustration of the confidence which the Rangers put in their own powers than the fact that Hall set about his task with only eighteen men. There were at least five hundred men directly and indirectly engaged in the Taylor-Sutton feud at the time.

Shortly before our arrival in the county, a despicable murder was committed by members of the Sutton party. They went at midnight to the residence of Dr. Brazell, an educated, refined old gentleman, dragged him from a sick bed in the presence of his wife and daughter, and murdered him in cold blood. At the same time, they killed his son.

Hall, in a report to Adjutant-General Steele, dated December 16, 1876, wrote:

"I am confident of arresting the murderers of Dr. Brazell and his son. I hold now thirty-one murder indictments and know where I can get the men. All of these men have friends all over the county, as more than half the county is mixed up in the matter. They are so involved in deeds of blood that they cannot afford to have any member of the brotherhood sent to prison. The people are completely terrorized and cowed by the assassins and cut-throats who got their hands in, shedding blood during the Taylor-Sutton troubles, then joined so-called vigilant associations, and are now killing off witnesses and intimidating juries by threats of violence, so that it is impossible to secure a conviction."

It was about this time that Hall first met Judge Henry Clay

Pleasants, the District Judge whose district took in DeWitt County.

"You do your part," said the old Judge to Hall, "and I will see that the courts deal justice. Together, we can bring order out of chaos."

Judge Pleasants was of an old Virginia family—one of the F. F. Vs.—and was a courtly, dignified, delightful gentleman. He was not only a strict and impartial Judge, but he was as brave as a lion, too; and the latter quality was perhaps needed quite as much as the others at that time in DeWitt County.

On the evening of December 22, 1876, Lieutenant Hall rode out from Clinton to our camp, near the town, and told us to saddle up to go on a little scout with him.

"We won't go far," he said, "so you needn't take any blankets. We'll be back to-night."

It was drizzling at the time and very cold for that part of Texas. Two of the men were sick and were in a house in the town for shelter, so that only sixteen men went with the Lieutenant. As we rode along through the dark night, Hall told us that we were going to arrest seven men who had just been indicted for murder of the Brazells. He said that one of the indicted men was Joseph Sitterlee, Deputy Marshal and Deputy Sheriff of DeWitt County, and that Sitterlee was being married that night. We were going to the wedding at the house of the bride's father and expected to find all of the Sutton gang there.

When we reached a point about two hundred yards from the house, we dismounted and Hall told us we were probably going to have a pretty hot fight in a few minutes. He produced a bottle of whiskey and we each drank to the success of the undertaking. Then we silently stole toward the house. As we got nearer, we could see that it was brightly lighted up and that a dance was in progress. A fiddle was squeaking, and through the windows we could see the dancers. A great many men were in the house, which was a large double one, with a gallery on each side of it.

Hall placed his men in a wide circle all around the building. I was put right in front of it in a shaft of light which streamed from one of the windows. As soon as I discovered this fact, I stepped a yard or two to one side, out of the light. At the ends of the long porches Hall placed four men with double-barrelled shotguns. Then he made a rapid round of the lines to see that every man was in his place. He came to me and asked, pleasantly:

"Well, how's the fighting Quaker getting on?"

"Bully," I said.

"Good. Now don't let a man escape past you. I'm going into the house in a few minutes and then there is going to be fun. Some of them will try to get away, but if they come your way, stop them. Don't shoot unless you have to."

He disappeared in the darkness and I waited. In a few minutes, I saw the tall form of the Lieutenant pass in at the open door of the room where the dance was going on. He held a carbine in his hand. Instantly the music stopped and I could see many six-shooters being flourished in the air. The women screamed and there was a sudden rushing to and fro of men and the sound of angry voices.

"Do you want any one here, Hall?" called out Sitterlee, as he confronted the officer at the doorway.

"Yes," cried Hall, in a loud voice; "I want seven men for murder. I want you and William Meadows, the Marshal of Cuero, and Dave Augustine and Jake Ryan and William Cox and Frank Heister and Charles Heidrichs, all charged with the murder of Dr. Brazell and his son and indicted this day."

At these words the uproar redoubled and Hall was forced back on the gallery which divided the two parts of the house.

Meadows raised his voice above the others and, going up to Hall, demanded, excitedly:

"How many men have you got?"

"Seventeen, counting myself," said Hall, calmly.

"Well, we've got over seventy and we'll fight it out," roared Meadows.

"Yes, yes; let's fight it out, let's fight it out!" came a chorus.

"That's the talk," shouted Hall in a delighted tone. "Move out your women and children and be quick about it. "I'll give you three minutes to get them out of the way. We don't want to kill them, but it is as much as I can do to restrain my men. We came here for a fight and we want it."

A silence followed the bold words.

"Get ready, men," Hall yelled to the Rangers. "You with the shot-guns sweep the porches when I give the word. The rest of you shoot to kill. They're going to move out their women and children and then we'll have it."

Meadows was crying with anger and mortification by this time.

"We don't want to kill you all," he blurted out.

"Then give me your gun—quick now!" said Hall, sharply, reaching out his hand and disarming Meadows before that worthy knew well what had happened.

Hall was quick to follow up his advantage. He grabbed six-shooters out of men's hands, right and left, and called to two of the Rangers to come up and help him take them. In two minutes, a dozen men were disarmed and the Rangers were forcing their way through the crowd, taking guns and pistols as they went.

Not a shot was fired, and in five minutes we had disarmed the entire Sutton gang.

"Are you going to take us to-night?" asked Sitterlee. "You might let us finish our dance out. I've just been married."

"All right," said Hall. "Finish the dance if you want to, but if any man tries to get away, we'll kill him, as certain as you stand there. We'll take you to town at daylight."

The dance was resumed and we stood guard around the house all night, going in, two at a time, to eat some of the wedding-supper. I observed that the prettiest girls there were the ones who seemed to take a pride in dancing with the accused murderers.

I neglected to say that, at the beginning of the rumpus, one fat old fellow came plunging out of the house wildly in the dark and ran as hard as he could straight for me. I punched him in the stomach with the end of my carbine, and he doubled up and turned like a hare back to the house. This man, it turned out later, was the "parson" who had performed the marriage ceremony.

Soon after dawn, we took our seven prisoners, all mounted, to Clinton and put them in a room in the jail there, two of the Rangers remaining in the room with them to guard them and four other Rangers standing guard outside the biulding. We had three reliefs of six men each, four hours during the day and four hours at night. Hall had informed all at the dance, as we took the prisoners away, that we would kill the prisoners first if there was any attempt at a rescue and that afterwards we would attend to the rescuing party.

It was hard work, guarding those men in the Clinton jail, which was a little old rickety building, so on the second day Hall removed them to the upper floor of the fine big court-house, where it was much easier to look after them.

Habeas corpus proceedings were begun in their behalf in a few days and the Court sat for a week hearing them. Every day the court-room was crowded with members of both the Taylor and Sutton parties, but as we were careful to disarm every man who entered the building, there was no clash.

As the proceedings drew to a close, we received information that the members of the Sutton gang were determined that their seven comrades, under no circumstances should be sent to jail. Judge Pleasants received several anonymous letters in which the threat was made that he would be shot and killed if he decided against the accused murderers. Hall decided to run no chances, and accordingly sent for more Rangers. They arrived the night before the day Judge Pleasants was to render his decision. With the reinforcements, we had thirty Rangers, enough to take care of every "bad man" in the county, if need be.

When court was called to order, the room was crowded with men, and everywhere it was whispered that Judge Pleasants would be shot if he decided against the prisoners and sent them to prison to await trial, instead of admitting them to bail.

The old Judge took his seat on the bench amid a profound silence. One could feel the suppressed excitement in the court-room and see it reflected in the faces of the spectators. Just before the Judge arose to give his decision, six of the Rangers stepped up to the bench and stood on either side of the Judge. I was one of the three on his right and was next to his side. Like the other five men, I had my carbine in my hand and, like the others, I threw a cartridge into the breech and cocked the gun in plain sight of all in the court-room. Then we stood at "ready" while Judge Pleasants addressed the crowd of men in the room. With supreme dignity he stood and looked at them for a full minute before he spoke. Then he said, in a calm, distinct voice whose every tone carried conviction:

"The time has arrived for me to announce my decision in this case. I shall do so without fear or favor, solely upon the evidence as it has been presented. This county is and has been for years a reproach to the fair name of the State of Texas. Over it have roamed bands of lawless men, committing awful outrages, murdering whom they pleased, shooting down men from ambush in the most cowardly manner possible. Here in this very room, listening to me now, are murderers who long ago should have been hanged. I do not speak of the prisoners at the bar, but of you who yet are free. You are murderers, bushwhackers, midnight assassins.

"Some of you have dared to threaten me with cowardly anonymous letters, and I have had to bring State soldiers into this court of justice. I learn that you have blamed the Sheriff of this county for calling upon the Rangers to assist in restoring order. No, it was not the Sheriff who had the Rangers sent here; it was I. I called for them and I am going to see that they remain here in this county until it is as peaceful and law-abiding as any in the State—as quiet and orderly as any in the Union. I tell you now, beware! The day of reckoning is surely coming. It is close at hand. When you deal with the Texas Rangers, you deal with men who are fearless in the discharge of their duty and who will surely conquer you.

"I shall send these men at the bar to jail to await trial for as wicked and cowardly a murder as ever disgraced this State. It is but the beginning. Others will soon follow them. The reign of the lawless in DeWitt County is at an end!"

Never shall I forget how the gray-haired old Judge's eyes flashed and how his fine voice rang as he pronounced these words. Angry looks came into the faces of scores of men in the courtroom, but they knew better than to make any demonstration.

"Lieutenant Hall, clear the room, sir," ordered Judge Pleasants, when he concluded. In a very few minutes the order was obeyed, and men who had come to Clinton determined to create trouble were leaving the town, thoroughly cowed.

It was the beginning of the end of their power in the county, and they knew it.

Chapter XIX

JOHN WESLEY HARDIN, THE WORST OF THE "BAD MEN"

From that time, the Rangers were exceedingly active in DeWitt County, and hundreds of arrests were made. The desperadoes could no longer find shelter there. A guard of four men went with Judge Pleasants when he travelled through the county, and wherever he held court Rangers were always present. Gradually the worst characters in the county were either jailed or run out, and in a few weeks' time order was restored and the long-standing feud was a thing of the past.

January 26, 1877, Captain McNelly, who had become an invalid, resigned his command, and the Ranger troop was reorganized at Victoria, under command of Lee Hall.

On the day we were reorganized, I had some words with Rector, and we both pulled our six-shooters and were about to fire, when Armstrong and one or two others got between us and we were disarmed and put under arrest. We decided to fight a duel at daylight the next morning with six-shooters, beginning at twenty paces and advancing. It was to be a duel to the death.

That afternoon, I was standing on the street in Victoria with Griffin, when a doctor drove up in his buggy and got down. He looked at us for a moment closely and then asked:

"Say, aren't you boys feeling a little under the weather?"

We both said we were feeling ill. I had been ill for two days, but had thought little of it.

"Well," said the doctor, "I believe you both have the measles. The best thing for you to do is to go and get a big drink of whiskey and hot water and go to bed at the hotel. I'll come around later and see how you are getting on."

We followed his directions, and that night I was delirious. I was out of my head for two days, and on the third Rector came around and we made up our quarrel and shook hands.

The reader may be curious to know why we were going to fight and what caused our quarrel. Strange as it may seem, I cannot remember at this time why we quarrelled. I only know that we had words about something at camp, but what that something was I do not remember. It is only another illustration of the reckless kind of fellows we were in those good old days of Ranger life, ready to fight at the twitching of a finger, for little or nothing.

After the reorganization of the Rangers, we returned to De-Witt County and continued to arrest men for whom indictments were found. We also went into other near-by counties, everywhere arresting desperadoes. I have copies of the reports made to the Adjutant-General, and find in them that in a little more than two months we arrested over eleven hundred men.

We had no fights and so did not kill anyone. We couldn't get into a fight in those days, because we couldn't find any men who would fight us. We had been so uniformly successful and had come out victors so often against heavy odds that whenever we ran across desperate characters, so called, they would submit at once. It became too tame to be interesting—certainly too void of excitement to be worth recording. I shall, therefore, depart from the continued narrative of the Ranger life and only give those incidents which were of extraordinary interest and importance.

The arrest of Ham White, stage robber, was one of these. Captain Hall personally made that arrest.

Ham White was a genuine Knight of the Road. He was as fine in his methods as ever Claude Duval, that prince of highwaymen, dared to be. It is related by Macaulay how, at the head of his troop, Duval, "stopped a lady's coach, in which there was a booty of four hundred pounds; how he took only one hundred, and suffered the fair owner to ransom the rest by dancing a coranto with him on the hearth."

Now, although Ham White probably never "danced a coranto" in his life, and wouldn't have known a "coranto" if he had seen one, he was much more gallant than Duval, for he refused to rob ladies at all. He hadn't any "troop," but worked absolutely alone.

He did not stop ladies' coaches, but held up the regular stage coaches with Wells, Fargo Express boxes and Uncle Sam's mail-bags on them. Twice in one day in the latter part of March, 1877, White robbed the stage coaches between Austin and San Antonio. He did not get much booty from the first coach, so he waited for the other. It was filled with passengers and a guard was riding on it, but Ham White with his six-shooters was a match for them all, and they surrendered without a struggle.

He made the passengers get out and cut open the United States mail-bags and hand him the registered packages. While they were thus engaged, White discoursed to them upon the enormity of their action.

"Don't you know how wicked it is to rob the mailbags?" he asked, facetiously. "I certainly would make a complaint against you, but I haven't the time to fool around the courts as a witness."

A man who handed all his money over to White—some three hundred dollars—said to him:

"I should like to get my watch back, as it was a present to me from my brother, who is dead."

"I would not think of taking it from you, if that is the case," said White. "Here, take this ten dollars, so that you will have enough to live on, a day or so, when you reach San Antonio."

To a lady who was one of the passengers, he said:

"Madam, there is no reason for your alarm. I can assure you, I have no intention of taking a cent from you."

To the stage-driver he said:

"I'd like to swap my horse for that off-leader of yours. My horse is really a better animal, but yours is fresher, and I may have to do some fast riding when I leave you."

Of course, the trade was made, and it was because of the exchange of horses that White was captured. The stage-horse he took had a broken shoe and, consequently, was easy to track. Captain Hall was informed, that evening, of the robbery, and early the next morning took up White's trail at the place where he had held up the stage-coach. With three of the Rangers, Hall tracked White for a day and a half. That brought the pursuing party to Luling.

In the livery-stable there, Hall found his man. The three Rangers were at dinner at the hotel, when Hall met White in the stable. White reached for his pistols, but Hall threw himself on the man and bore him to the floor. They had a rough-and-tumble fight, at the end of which Hall was sitting on the helpless White and relieving him of $4,000 in gold.

White was tried and received ninety-nine years in a military prison, for robbing the United States mails. It turned out that White was a near relative of Secretary of the Navy Goff, under President Hayes, and Hayes pardoned the stage-robber. It was the last act of Hayes' official life.

White returned to Southwest Texas and made threats that he

would have Captain Hall's life, but Hall started out to find him and White disappeared. He next turned up in Colorado under the name of H. W. Burton, and began robbing stages between Lake City and Alamosa. Then, with ten or twelve men, he robbed trains in Colorado. He was caught and again sentenced to life imprisonment, but on an appeal escaped on a legal technicality. He disappeared for a while, but finally was arrested in Ohio for killing the man who had killed his father. He escaped from the Columbus, Ohio, jail and the last heard of him, he was robbing stages in California, in 1892, and always alone. He has been confounded many times with the notorious Black Bart, but was far more daring than that "knight of the road."

In April, 1877, I was one of nine Rangers who guarded Frank Singleton in the little two-roomed jail in Beeville, prior to his execution for murder. He was the first of the murderers to be sentenced by Judge Pleasants, and it was important that the sentence of the Court should be carried out without a hitch. Singleton had a big following, and many threats were made that he would never be hanged. The date of his execution was fixed for April 27th.

He was as cool a man, under the circumstances, as I ever saw, and my experience as a Ranger and, many years later, as a New York newspaper reporter, brought me into personal contact with many condemned murderers. Singleton made an absurd will, a few days before his execution. In it he bequeathed his skin to the prosecuting attorney of the county, with the suggestion that it be stretched into a drumhead and beaten at the door of the courthouse every year, on the anniversary of his execution, "as a warning to evil-doers." The rest of his body he bequeathed to the doctors, to be used in the cause of science.

On the evening before the day of execution, nine more Rangers came to Beeville and joined us. That night I passed in Singleton's cell with him. Three other Rangers were also in the cell. The jail was a wooden affair and the Sheriff had chained Singleton to the floor. The chain was fastened to heavy iron shackles which were forged around the prisoner's ankles.

All night long I played "seven-up" with Singleton. We played for $10 a game—on trust. Singleton owed me $40 at the end of the games.

"I don't know where I'm going," said he; "but wherever it may be, I'll try and have that $40 for you by the time you come along."

When the sheriff came to remove the shackles from Singleton's feet, the murderer said:

"Sheriff, I wouldn't use those leg-irons again, if I were you."

"Why?" asked the Sheriff.

For answer, Singleton picked up the shackles and with his thumb-nail removed some soap from a crack in them, revealing how he had managed to saw them nearly in two.

"I'd have been away from here long ago," he said, "if it hadn't been for these Rangers. They watched me too closely. I had a file and a little saw and a bottle of nitric acid. I softened the iron with the acid and sawed away at night."

"Where are these tools?"

Singleton put his finger in a crack between the boards which made the inner wall of his cell and pulled up a string to which the saw, file and a bottle of acid were attached. He would not say how he obtained them, but he presented the file to me.

"You may keep that to remember me by," he said. "You may need it, some day, if you ever get into a fix like mine."

I thanked him, despite the rather dubious suggestiveness of his estimate of my character.

He was executed in front of the jail, and people came from all over the county to see him hanged. Many women and children were in the crowd. The Rangers formed a circle around the high scaffold and kept back the crowd. We made such a display of force that a scheme of his friends to rescue Singleton at the last moment was not attempted. He was smoking a cigar as he walked up the steep steps of the scaffold. The black-cap was put half on his head and then he threw the cigar away, saying:

"I reckon you and I'll go out at about the same time."

A few minutes later he was dangling at the end of the rope, dead.

John Wesley Hardin, of DeWitt County, was the worst of the "bad men" Texas produced in such numbers during the stormy reconstruction days. He was probably the worst desperado ever in Texas, at any time. When the Rangers captured him, late in August, 1877, he was known to have killed over a score of men. He himself placed the number at twenty-seven, "not counting Mexicans and niggers."

The name of John Wesley Hardin was dreaded from one end of Texas to the other. Let it be rumored that Hardin was in a county, and that county became panic-stricken. When he rode into a town, the town and all its inhabitants were at his mercy, and hastened to do his bidding. If any person dared to thwart his will, another "killing" was added to Hardin's list. All the other "bad men" were as much afraid of John Wesley Hardin as peaceable citizens were afraid of them. He was a marvelous shot with a six-shooter. He could shoot with his left hand as well as with his right. He could take a six-shooter in each hand and put all twelve bullets in a playing-card at twenty yards with lightning rapidity. He could handle his favorite weapon as a juggler handles painted balls. He could twirl a six-shooter around his finger, by the trigger-guard, so rapidly that it looked like a wheel and then, at the word, fire and hit the mark. He could fire a Winchester repeating rifle so rapidly that a continuous stream of fire came from the muzzle and four or five empty shells from the ejecter were in the air at the same time, falling at different heights, to the ground.

He killed men on the slightest provocation, and on no provocation at all. He never forgave an injury, and to incur his displeasure was simply suicide.

Out of the many tales of Hardin which were current in Texas, I select two or three which I know to be true.

On one occasion, he met a sewing-machine agent in the country. The agent was driving a wagon in which were two or three sewing machines. Hardin made the agent take one of the machines from the wagon, place it in the dusty road and sew on it. The desperado took off his jacket, ripped it up the back, and made the agent sew it up again. He amused himself in this way for two hours and then sent the agent about his business with the remark:

"I'm pretty good-natured to-day, so I won't kill you if you get away quick."

One day, Hardin found himself short of money. He came to a country store where a number of men were congregated. He told them he wanted to get money by raffling off his horse and saddle. The chances were two dollars each. The men were afraid to refuse to take chances, and some of them tried to curry favor with the noted desperado by taking two or three chances apiece. Hardin took the money and told them to begin throwing the dice. While they were doing so, Hardin walked out, mounted his horse and rode away. Not a single of his victims dared follow him.

At Cuero, one day, he was in a saloon, drinking. He stepped to the door and saw a stranger sitting on a dry-goods box, two blocks away.

"I'll bet you the drinks I can kill that fellow the first shot with my revolver," said Hardin to a companion.

The bet was accepted and Hardin pulled his six-shooter and fired. The man fell dead. Hardin went into the saloon and took his drink, as calmly as though nothing unusual had happened.

A sheriff got the drop on Hardin once and arrested him. He kept the outlaw covered with his six-shooter and told him to hand over his revolvers. Hardin took his pistol and, holding it by the barrel, handed it, butt first, to the sheriff. The sheriff extended his hand for the weapon, but just as his fingers were closing on it, Hardin gave it a sudden flirt and a twist and fired, sending a ball through the sheriff's heart.

At another time, he was arrested and five negro soldiers were taking him to jail. In the night, Hardin managed to get his hands untied. He crept behind the man on guard and stunned him with a blow from a stick. Then he deliberately murdered all five soldiers.

He began murdering men when he was only fifteen years old. He grew into a short, stocky man, of great activity and strength. He was a perfect rider. His face was broad. He had little, pig-like eyes, which had the glitter and very much the expression of the eyes of a rattlesnake. They were ever moving here and there and were not quiet for a moment. This habit of glancing continually right and left and behind him, was caused by the constant outlook he had to maintain against surprise, for he had many bitter enemies who would not have hesitated to kill him from behind, although they dared not face him.

Hardin's parents were good, simple folk, his father being a preacher of the frontier sort, who mingled the occupation of ranch-man with that of his sacred calling, because his pay as a preacher was never sufficient to support his family. His intention was to make a preacher of his son, and the name John Wesley was given him in memory of the great founder of Methodism. The son turned out to be the heaviest cross ever a preacher was called upon to bear, but despite the boy's wickedness, he was always beloved by his parents.

Another illustration of his cold-blooded character came to me in Texas, well authenticated. One night Hardin was awakened in a lodging-house by the snoring of a man on the other side of a thin wooden partition. Having fixed the precise point where the sleeper lay, Hardin fired through the partition, killed him, and then turned over and slumbered peacefully for the rest of the night.

A few months before Hardin's capture and conviction, a young man was walking on the streets in Cuero with a young woman to whom he was engaged to be married. The couple met a noted bully, who was out on a periodical tear. He met and passed them, and then deliberately turned and shot the young man dead. A more wanton murder was never committed, for the two had not exchanged a word, and never saw each other before. Nothing was done with the assassin in the fued-ridden country. He was not even arrested. The brother of the victim was so enraged when he learned of the murder that he started out with a shot-gun, swearing he would kill the assassin or be killed himself.

While he was hunting through the various saloons for him, he met Hardin, who inquired his business. The young man, almost beside himself, explained.

"You can't work it," said Hardin, with a warning shake of the head; "that fellow'll get the drop on you quicker'n lightning."

"I don't care; he murdered my brother, and I'll never rest until I shoot him."

"Well," said Hardin, "I'll go along and see that you get a square deal."

At this moment, the young man caught sight of the miscreant, on the other side of the narrow street. He took deliberate aim and fired, but was so excited he missed his man. The desperado whirled around like a flash and had the drop on the young man before he knew his danger.

"So you're looking for me, are you?" he asked with a grin; "wal, I'll give you just two minutes to say your prayers in."

And as he held his pistol on a dead level, while the trembling youth could do nothing but stand in his tracks, helplessly awaiting his fate. But the bully failed to note another figure, standing a few paces behind the youth, calmly watching the proceedings. Before the two minutes had expired, Hardin fired and the other desperado rolled over with a bullet in his brain.

Among the many deaths inflicted by Hardin's pistol or Winchester, this is the only one for which an impartial jury would have acquitted him.

CHAPTER XX

HARDIN A PRISONER—THE OLD BAND DISBANDED

When the Rangers began to make things so hot for the desperadoes in and near DeWitt County, Hardin disappeared. Try as we might, we could learn nothing of his whereabouts. He was a prize worth capturing, too, not only because he was such a notorious desperado, but also because the State offered a reward of $4,000 for him, dead or alive. Connected with the Rangers, and on the pay-rolls, were two or three men who were only known to the Captain. They were the detectives of our force. One of these men was John Duncan.

By order of Captain McNelly, Duncan had, months before, undertaken to find John Wesley Hardin. To this end, Duncan hired the ranch adjoining that owned by Hardin's father, the preacher. The Ranger detective cultivated the friendship of the old man, but did it with such deliberation and naturalness that his identity or purpose was never suspected.

For days, weeks, and months the two met in the evening, smoked their pipes, and talked over matters such as naturally occurred to them; but never once was reference made to John Wesley Hardin, the son. The detective, however, was biding his time, and it was not until five months had passed that the chance for which he was waiting came. One afternoon, just as it was growing dark, Mr. Hardin remarked that he had a letter to mail, and would walk to the postoffice, which was in a grocery store at the junction of the highway, half a mile away.

"I may as well take a stroll with you," said the other, rising to his feet. Hardin was glad to have him, and they entered the store together. Hardin asked for a pen with which to direct the letter, which was written in lead-pencil and enclosed in an envelope. The postmaster handed him a pen, and Hardin began writing the name slowly and with great care. Just before he finished, the pipe of the detective went out, and he leaned over the shoulder of the unsuspecting Hardin, to get a match. As he did so, he gave one quick glance at the envelope. It was enough, for he read the name and address and was sure to remember them.

Duncan and Hardin walked home together, conversing on the way on various matters. A few days later, Duncan said he would have to go to St. Louis, to see some cattle-men there. Instead of going to St. Louis, however, Duncan went straight to San Antonio, where he met John Armstrong, Charley McKinney, and two other Rangers. The party at once started for Florida, for the address on the letter the old man had sent was "William Jones," at a little place near Pensacola, Florida.

They arrived at Pensacola, August 18th. Duncan took the train for the little station to which the letter was addressed. He saw Hardin at work in a field on a farm, but passed him by without apparent notice. Duncan came back to Pensacola. He had taken the telegraph-operator at the little station into his confidence, however, and had arranged with him to send a despatch notifying him when Hardin should next take the train for a station near Pensacola. The operator told Duncan that Hardin was in the habit of taking this train about once a week, as he was paying attentions to a farmer's daughter at the second station.

On Saturday, August 23rd, Duncan received the telegram he expected, and he and the four Rangers went at once to a point up the railroad where Hardin's train was scheduled to stop. When the train arrived, Armstrong entered the car where Hardin sat, walking in at the forward end. Hardin and a companion were the only occupants of the car. Another of the Rangers entered the car at the rear door and took the seat immediately behind Hardin and his friend. The other officers remained outside, near the platforms.

Hardin paid no attention to Armstrong and the other Ranger until Armstrong reached the place where the desperado was sitting. Then Armstrong looked Hardin straight in the eye and said: "How are you, John Wesley Hardin?"

With a motion as quick as a flash, Hardin threw back his hand for his six-shooter; but the Ranger who was behind him was expecting this, and caught the outlaw's arm and hung on to it.

Hardin's companion drew his six-shooter, however, and Armstrong immediately put a bullet in his head. Then a fight with Hardin began all over the car. He kicked and bit like a wildcat, trying his best all the while to get at his revolver. It took five minutes to handcuff and disarm him.

A TEXAS RANGER

Without waiting for requisition papers, or even to notify the Florida officers of the capture, Armstrong and his party started for Texas. They actually kidnapped Hardin, and were going through Alabama before they were stopped. Then an officious lawyer got an order from an Alabama court, which delayed the party twenty-four hours. The news that John Wesley Hardin was on the train drew great crowds, all through Louisiana and Eastern Texas, to the stations. As the party approached Austin, the crowds grew larger and larger. In Austin itself, the streets near the railroad station were filled with a crowd and it was whispered that a lot of DeWitt County desperadoes were there to rescue Hardin.

This rumor reached the ears of the Rangers who had gathered in Austin, and they telegraphed to Armstrong. The consequence was that Hardin was taken off the train on the outskirts of Austin and conveyed to the jail by the Rangers on horseback before the crowd at the depot knew what had happened.

Hardin was tried on one of the many indictments against him, and found guilty of murder in the second degree! The Governor had said that he would pardon Hardin if he was not sentenced to be hanged, and have him tried on others of the eighteen murder indictments against him until a jury could be found who would find him guilty of murder in the first degree, but this was not done. Hardin was sentenced to the State penitentiary at Huntsville for twenty-five years. When he went to jail he swore that if he outlived his sentence, he would hunt down every man concerned in his capture and kill all.

Armstrong and his four companions received $800 each from the State for capturing Hardin. They regretted, later, that they had not turned him over to the Louisiana authorities, for there was a reward of $12,000 for him in Louisiana, for murders committed there.

Strange as it may seem, Hardin was pardoned by Governor Hogg, of Texas, in 1893. What possible reason there could be for granting a pardon to such an unspeakable villain, it is difficult to conceive; but certain it is that by the Governor's action the man was set free. He studied law while in the penitentiary, and when he was set at liberty he announced his intention of practising at the bar.

For awhile after his release he was on his good behavior, but soon he showed signs of going back to his old life. He went to

El Paso, and on the night of May 2, 1895, "held up" the "Gem" gambling-house there in a most sensational manner. He played faro until he lost several hundred dollars. Then he suddenly drew his six-shooter and, pointing it at the head of the faro-dealer, said:

"You are too cute for me,——you! Now just hand me over the money I paid for my chips and all the rest you have in the drawer."

The dealer, a man named Baker, handed over the money without a word and Hardin walked out of the place. Hardin left the town, but returned in August of the same year to see a woman who lived there. He found, on his arrival, that the woman had been arrested a few days before, by a policeman named Sellman. Hardin threatened to run Sellman out of the town.

Two nights later—August 19, 1895—Constable Sellman, the father of the policeman, walked into a bar-room where Hardin was shaking dice. As soon as Hardin saw Sellman, he whirled around and put his hand to his hip to draw his six-shooter. Sellman was quicker than he, however, and sent a bullet crashing through the desperado's head. As Hardin was falling, Sellman sent two more bullets through his heart.

The worst of all the "bad men" of Texas thus died "with his boots on," as he had often sworn he would die.

I should like to go on and tell, in detail, all the exploits of the Rangers, but, interesting as it is to me to recall those exciting days, I fear that the reader has supped too full of horrors already. I should like to recount how Captain Hall and his men rounded up a great band of Mexican bandits, who in 1878, arranged to invade Texas under General Escobedo, the man who shot Maximilian; how we came near taking retaliatory measures and invading Mexico in force, for Governor Hubbard threatened to issue a proclamation calling for fifty thousand men; how we made a forced march of 250 miles in three and a half days, from El Paso to the stronghold of Escobedo's men, and succeeded in arresting him and his followers.

All these matters are of much reminiscent interest to me, but to give them with proper detail would make too long a story. The killing of Sam Bass and his notorious gang in August, 1878, by Lee Hall and others of the Rangers; the final breaking up of every band of desperadoes in Texas; the establishment of law and order where formerly outlaws governed; the making of the great State into an orderly, prosperous country, where life and property is as safe as in New York, is the record of the Rangers. It is a record of which the survivors of the old troop have good reason to be proud.

I say "the survivors," for the great majority of the old comrades I loved are dead. Charley McKinney, as I have told, was murdered by a man whom he tried to arrest. The murderer was afterward hanged in San Antonio. Every little while, I hear of another of the Rangers passing away. McNelly died of consumption, early in 1878.

King Fisher and Ben Thompson, the latter having a "killing" record of some thirty odd men, were both killed in one night by William R. Simms, a gambler of San Antonio. They entered the variety theatre owned by Simms, with the expressed purpose of "cleaning it out." Simms, who was mild-mannered and gentlemanly, went to the box where the two "man-killers" were, and expostulated with them. Thompson called him a vile name and "reached" for his revolver.

In an instant, Simms shot him through the head. Thompson, as he fell, managed to fire his pistol twice into the floor, although a bullet had passed through his brain. Fisher had his hand on his pistol, but before he could use it, Simms shot him through the heart. Simms was tried and acquitted, the plea being self-defense. I saw Simms on my last visit to Texas. Never have I met a more entertaining man. He dislikes greatly to talk of the killing of Fisher and Thompson. It made him for a time the "mark" for every aspiring "bad man" who went to San Antonio. They got drunk and straightway made up their minds that they would kill Simms, the man who killed two men in one night. Simms was forced to shoot three of these rash cow-boys who came to kill him.

"I got tired of it," he said to me. "I wanted to live in peace, but they wouldn't let me. Sometimes I would go up to New England and hunt out some quiet, retired village where I might be at rest, but, although I went under an assumed name at such times, my identity was sure to be discovered and then I was looked upon with suspicion.

"I was in one of these little New England towns, one summer, and was enjoying myself greatly in a quiet way, when one day the barber who was shaving me said:

" 'You don't seem to me like such a bad man, Mr. Simms.'

"I jumped so that the barber almost cut my throat with his razor.

" 'Who told you my name was Simms and that I was a bad man?' I demanded.

"He said that an agent for a laundry company had told him that I had killed twenty-four men. He said that the laundry-agent was formerly the county clerk in San Antonio. I knew that part of the story was a lie, and I started out to look for the laundry-man. I couldn't find him, and I returned to my hotel. Then I noticed that men gathered in little groups and eyed me as though I were some wild animal. Presently, a young man stepped up to me and said:

" 'I should like to have you patronize our laundry, sir.'

"I jumped for him and grabbed him by the collar. He grew as white as one of the shirts his laundry did up.

" 'So you're the man who has told everyone that I killed twenty-four men!' I shouted. 'Who are you, anyway? I know you were never the county clerk at San Antonio.'

" 'I—I worked in the county clerk's office,' he stammered, 'and I really did hear you had killed twenty-four men.'

" 'Young man,' I said, 'you and I are going to take a little walk out into that cornfield over there. Only one of us is coming back again. I think I'll be the one to come back.'

"He begged for his life, and I told him I'd let him off if he'd go to everyone he had talked to about me and tell each one that he had been lying. He did it, but I came away in a few days. The place had lost all its charm for me."

The old company of Rangers was at an end when Captain Hall resigned, in 1880. I resigned late in 1878, and returned to Philadelphia. I thought I had seen enough adventure for a man of twenty-two. I tried to live a quiet, civilized life, but the tameness of an existence in the city was more than I could stand and, in 1881, I started West again, this time for Colorado. I became a prospector and miner in the Rockies, and put in nearly three more years of wild life in the mining-camps and the mountains. Some day I may tell of those days, for they were filled with adventure.

It is a relief to put on paper the record of the free, out-door existence of by-gone years. I am glad I have done it, for it is well that the history of McNelly's and Hall's Texas Rangers should live after we who made up that body have passed away.